LUTHER

Selected Political Writings

LUTHER
Selected Political Writings

EDITED AND WITH AN INTRODUCTION BY

J. M. PORTER

FORTRESS PRESS/PHILADELPHIA

The texts selected for inclusion in this book are all excerpted from the American Edition of *Luther's Works*.

The Freedom of a Christian
Copyright © 1957 by Muhlenberg Press
now Fortress Press

*To the Christian Nobility of the German Nation
Concerning the Reform of the Christian Estate*
Copyright © 1966 by Fortress Press

Temporal Authority: To What Extent It Should Be Obeyed
Copyright © 1962 by Fortress Press

Admonition to Peace: A Reply to the Twelve Articles of the Peasants in Swabia
Copyright © 1967 by Fortress Press

Against the Robbing and Murdering Hordes of Peasants
Copyright © 1967 by Fortress Press

An Open Letter on the Harsh Book Against the Peasants
Copyright © 1967 by Fortress Press

Whether Soldiers, Too, Can Be Saved
Copyright © 1967 by Fortress Press

On War Against the Turk
Copyright © 1967 by Fortress Press

Dr. Martin Luther's Warning to His Dear German People
Copyright © 1971 by Fortress Press

Library of Congress Catalog Card Number 74–76931

ISBN 0–8006–1079–2

4282B74   Printed in U.S.A.   1–1079

CONTENTS

64946

INTRODUCTION

The Political Thought of Martin Luther[1]
by J. M. Porter

I

Luther is a complicated and controversial thinker. He wrote, as did his great mentor Augustine, in response to vital issues and controversies of his day. Particularly in the realm of political thought, one can find no systematic work or essay by Luther unconnected with a political crisis or problem of the time. Even the Reformation doctrines of the priesthood of all believers and justification by faith are presented in essays directed toward a contemporary controversy or topic. The titles found in this volume are indicative of the *genre* in which Luther wrote.

Controversy about the significance of Luther's political thought continues to exist. Luther has been called by some critics a precursor of the rise of National Socialism and an advocate of the "religion of the state." Other less extreme interpreters have argued that Luther's radical separation of the "two realms" or kingdoms—church authority and temporal authority—and the emphasis placed on the divine source of temporal authority lead to an "unqualified endorsement of state power" and to a greater fear of anarchy than of tyranny.[2] Although the deep religious convictions of Luther are not doubted, it has been argued that he could never reconcile his fundamental mysticism with the practical and political tasks of establishing the reformed churches, and, as a consequence, his religious and political doctrines were fundamentally inconsistent.[3] Some interpreters have argued that Luther developed two irreconcilable ethics: "He places

---

[1] The author is indebted to F. M. Barnard, University of Western Ontario, for helpful discussions and commentary on the Introduction. Notes on the chapters which follow this Introduction are to be found at the back of the book.
[2] Reinhold Niebuhr, *Christian Realism and Political Problems* (New York: Scribner's, 1953), p. 127. See also, Jacques Maritain, *Three Reformers: Luther, Descartes, Rousseau* (New York: Scribner's, 1950), pp. 21–22; J. N. Figgis, *Studies of Political Thought from Gerson to Grotius, 1414–1625* (Cambridge: Cambridge University Press, 1916), lecture 3, "Luther and Machiavelli."
[3] J. W. Allen, *A History of Political Thought in the Sixteenth Century* (London: Methuen, 1928), p. 16.

a perfectionist private ethic in juxtaposition to a realistic, not to say cynical official ethic."[4] It is not surprising, then, to find general assessments of Luther and his significance which are less than favorable. Ernst Troeltsch concludes:

> From the political and social point of view, the significance of Lutheranism for the modern history of civilization lies in its connection with reactionary parties: from the religious and scientific standpoint its significance lies in the development of a philosophical theology, which is blended with a religious mysticism and "inward" spirituality, but which, from the ethical point of view, is quite remote from the problems of modern political and social life.[5]

Other interpreters of Luther have found themes of enduring significance in Luther's political thought. It has been argued, for example, that Luther's doctrine of the "two kingdoms" has been of great value in the development of Western political thought and practice. The radical separation of temporal authority from man's ultimate end in the kingdom of God emphasizes the limited and lesser goals of the political sphere. Moreover, by the dedivinization of politics both the political and religious spheres are purified of the temptation toward political millenarianism and the worship of power. Likewise, Luther's theological doctrines, which stress the personal religious freedom of the Christian and the sanctity of the individual conscience, are said to have nourished several lasting political themes including various aspects of individualism. As an instance, these interpretations clearly suggest that the state's power over the individual is limited: temporal authority is never justified in trying to coerce the individual conscience. If active political resistance by the individual is not fully developed on these theological grounds, the right to disobey is. Luther's view of the sanctity of the individual conscience is also said to provide an impetus for religious toleration. The famous doctrines of justification by grace through faith and the priesthood of all believers had the significant consequence of placing a new stress on social-political action and responsibility since all callings can be used to serve God and neighbor and since the Christian works in the world willingly in faith, not for the selfish purpose of acquiring merit. The importance of all men's social and political

[4] Reinhold Niebuhr, *The Nature and Destiny of Man*, vol. 2 (New York: Scribner's, 1943), pp. 194-95.
[5] Ernst Troeltsch, *The Social Teachings of the Christian Churches*, trans. Olive Wyon, vol. 2 (London: Allen and Unwin, 1950), p. 577.

responsibilities is thus greatly increased. In sum, Luther's confidence in the individual conscience has become part of the cultural foundation of Western political life and systems.[6]

Where lies the truth in these various interpretations? As the selections in this volume indicate, Luther was an unsystematic and also a complicated thinker. An adequate understanding of him depends upon respecting the complicated character of his thought. For example, those commentators who characterize some aspects of Luther's thought as incoherent may have failed to understand his dialectical mode of reasoning. Gerhard Ebeling has observed that "Luther's thought always contains an antithesis, tension between strongly opposed but related polarities: theology and philosophy, the letter and Spirit, the law and the gospel, the double use of the law, person and works, faith and love, the kingdom of Christ and the kingdom of the world, man as a Christian and man in the world, freedom and bondage, God hidden and God revealed. . . ."[7] The historical contexts, as Luther perceived and explained them in his writings, and the development of his thought in response to the historical issues and events of his time provide further difficulties for understanding. Luther himself complains in *On War Against the Turk*: "But it is not fair to forget what the situation was then and what my grounds and reasons were, and to take my words and apply them to another situation where those grounds and reasons do not exist." The fact that Luther is not formally a political philosopher, at least in the sense that Machiavelli, Hobbes, or Rousseau are, is yet another complication. Unlike other political thinkers, Luther's perspective on politics is almost entirely theological—and this adds yet a further difficulty to understanding his political thought. This is not to say that his political views are hidden or undeveloped. Luther claims in *On War Against the Turk* that his political ideas are both novel and forthright: "No one had taught, no one had heard, and no one knew anything about temporal government,

---

[6] Karl Holl, *The Cultural Significance of the Reformation*, intro. by Wilhelm Pauck (New York: Meridian, 1959); Lee C. McDonald, *Western Political Theory: From Its Origins to the Present* (New York: Harcourt, Brace and World, 1968), pp. 238–39; W. D. J. Cargill Thompson, "Martin Luther and the 'Two Kingdoms'" in David Thomson, ed., *Political Ideas* (New York: Basic Books, 1966), pp. 27–47; Wilhelm Pauck, *The Heritage of the Reformation* (Glencoe, Ill.: Free Press, 1961), pp. 268–69; Harold J. Grimm, *The Reformation Era, 1500–1650* (New York: Macmillan, 1954), chap. 12.

[7] Gerhard Ebeling, *Luther: An Introduction to his Thought*, trans. R. A. Wilson (Philadelphia: Fortress Press, 1970), p. 25.

whence it came, what its office and work were, or how it ought to serve God." Nevertheless, in order to achieve an adequate understanding of Luther's political writings, one must approach them through his theology.

II

In *The Freedom of a Christian* and *To the Christian Nobility of the German Nation Concerning the Reform of the Christian Estate* Luther develops the three major Reformation doctrines which serve as the foundation for his political thought: the primacy of Scripture as the word of God, justification by faith, and the priesthood of all believers. Simultaneously, he contrasts these Reformation beliefs with those of the scholastic world and the papacy.

According to Luther, true Christianity can be restored only if the authority of the word of God as found in Scripture alone replaces that claimed by ecclesiastical institutions, canon law, and medieval theology. In the scholastic tradition, the church and reason had been authoritative interpreters and even sources for the word of God, but for Luther Scripture alone is the carrier. Although no expertise, no "reason" in the Thomistic and Aristotelian sense, is required for understanding and explaining the Bible, Luther's views on the accessibility of Scripture's meaning do not entail tolerance for any and all literalist interpretations. Rather, he cites Augustine's argument for the self-evident character of Scripture's meaning: "The truth itself lays hold on the soul and thus renders it able to judge most certainly of all things; however, the soul is not able to judge the truth, but is compelled to say with unnerving certainty that his is the truth."[8]

It is Luther's conviction that the justification by faith doctrine is the only biblical explanation of how man the sinner could be redeemed. God's grace is freely given to men of faith, and thus the spiritual torment of the sinner estranged from God is overcome. Such a man attains an inner state of liberty or freedom. It is the inner man, as Luther phrases it, who can be justified by grace through faith, and this justification cannot be achieved by good

---

[8] "The Babylonian Captivity," *Luther's Works*, vol. 36, *Word and Sacrament* II, trans. A. T. W. Steinhauser, revised by Frederick C. Ahrens and Abdel Ross Wentz (Philadelphia: Fortress Press, 1959), pp. 107–8. For Luther's attack on classical philosophy see Wilhelm Pauck, ed., *Luther: Lectures on Romans*, Library of Christian Classics, vol. 15 (Philadelphia: Westminster Press, 1961), pp. 235–37.

works or any other means. Luther elucidates these views in *The Freedom of a Christian*:

> It is clear, then, that a Christian has all that he needs in faith and needs no works to justify him; and if he has no need of works, he has no need of law; and if he has no need of the law, surely he is free from the law. It is true that "the law is not laid down for the just" (1 Tim. 1:9). This is that Christian liberty, our faith, which does not induce us to live in idleness or wickedness but makes the law and works unnecessary for any man's righteousness and salvation.

This Christian liberty is not meant by Luther to be a private state of mystic perfection free from sin nor is it meant to exempt one from good works. Sin expresses itself even in the lives of the saved, who are individually *justus et peccator simul* (righteous and sinner at once). The man with faith has turned from self to Christ, but no state of perfection is obtained in this mortal life. Likewise, Luther argues that we are not "wholly inner and perfectly spiritual men." The distinction between the inner and the outer man, faith and good works, is not meant to be a dichotomy or schism. The outer man has a responsibility to do good works, and he can do them because the inner man wishes "to serve God joyfully and without thought of gain." The works and tasks of a Christian on earth become "the freest of works, done only to please God and not to obtain righteousness." In short, works become the fruit of grace and not the means for acquiring it; the inner man, as the servant of all, bestows on the outer man Christian obligations and commandments for good works far surpassing those any law could require; the outer man can then freely and joyfully perform his tasks.

In understanding the central meaning of Luther's justification by faith doctrine it would be helpful to draw an analogy with the psychodynamic character of a friendship. No friendship can be healthy if the friends keep score on the amount or quality of favors, that is, good works, each has done for the other. By such score-keeping the other person becomes merely an instrument for favors rather than a person liked for himself. Similarly, a relationship with God that depends upon good works would become a type of spiritual accounting system rather than an open communion with God. For friendship to exist one must accredit, that is, have faith in, the good intention and will of the other person; otherwise, the other person's good intention becomes debunked as an action for or reaction to a favor. Faith in God, according to Luther, has this same dimension of trust or accreditation. The good intention of a friend must be truly accepted on its own, that is, as unmerited by any act of the receiver, or else the relationship will again become an instrumental one. Likewise, God's intention toward man is unmerited by the receiver and in theological language is called grace. A friendship that has these ingredients will be an intimate, open, and direct communion between two people. In Luther's mind, such a relationship can also exist with God if one understands truly that men are justified by grace through faith. Finally, where true friendship exists, kind acts or good works are done for each other joyfully without recourse to an accountant system of favors. Just so, a Christian joyfully fulfills his obligations for good works once his relationship with God has been properly established.

The third major religious doctrine of Luther is the priesthood of all believers. The accessibility of all men to the word of God in Scripture and to Christ through faith is an implicit theme in the other two doctrines. The priesthood of all believers explains this accessibility. All men can be priests because the grace of God is freely given to men. Consequently, the medieval role of the priest as dispenser of the sacraments is eliminated. Since all men have access to God, there should be no superiors and inferiors within an assigned religious hierarchy. The medieval priest is transformed in Luther's thought to an office holder who explains the word. He is not the carrier of a special power which makes him a necessary mediator for salvation. The sacraments are reduced in number from seven to the two with biblical sanctions, baptism and communion, a secondary status being accorded to penance. With the priesthood of all believers' doctrine Luther has substituted a radically egalitarian conception of the church for the medieval church with its gradations of authority and functions.

Personal, direct, and unhindered communion with God is strengthened through these three Reformation doctrines. In Luther's mind, any doctrines or institutions that hinder man's relation to God must be destroyed. Thus, the historical effect of his thought was to erode the ecclesiastical and ultimately cultural foundations of medieval society. While it is true that Luther acquiesces in the medieval social system, his religious desire to erase all barriers between the right relationship between God and man leads him to reject many of the political, intellectual, and religious tenets which constituted the medieval world.

The three great Reformation doctrines serve as a prism through which Luther examines all dimensions of human existence, including the political. In the process, Luther is able to transform and erode the medieval world while introducing new politically-significant ideas within the interstices of his theological arguments. Both features can be seen clearly in *To the Christian Nobility of the German Nation*. This work is a theological attack on the three "walls" which support the papacy, and it is also a call for specific reforms to eliminate corruption and various ecclesiastical abuses. The first wall is the papal claim, according to Luther, that spiritual power is superior to temporal power. Assessing this claim in terms of his priesthood of all believers principle, Luther disallows the distinction between clergy and laity, and he argues for the divinely ordained role of the temporal authorities to punish the wicked, including the clergy. The second and third walls, that only the pope can interpret Scripture and summon a council, are not supported by biblical authority. In attacking the three walls, Luther has clearly demolished the medieval principles of monarchy and hierarchy in ecclesiastical institutions. Also embedded in this theological attack on the papacy are political themes such as the nature of temporal authority, political obligation, and the relation of the church to temporal authority, which Luther develops in his later writings.

III

The major tenets of Luther's theology are presented by 1520 in such works as *On Christian Liberty* and *To the Christian Nobility of the German Nation*. It was 1523 before Luther presented a work which developed his political views into a coherent position, *Temporal Authority*.

In the first part of this work, he argues that there is biblical warrant for the divine origin of temporal authority independent of the church; he explains in the second part the limitations on temporal power; and in the third part he gives some pastoral advice to rulers. Undergirding Luther's political thought is the fundamental distinction he makes between the two kingdoms: "Here we must divide the children of Adam and all mankind into two classes, the first belonging to the kingdom of God, the second to the kingdom of the world. Those who belong to the kingdom of God are all the true believers." As Luther further explains, the non-Christians belong to "the kingdom of the world and are under law." Since Christians are few indeed and since the "whole world is evil," government with the sword and law punishes and restrains men to keep order in this world. Analogous to the relation between the inner and outer man, faith and good works, the Christian does not require temporal authority but he willingly serves his neighbor through it.

The importance of temporal authority is accentuated because it alone can preserve man from chaos and anarchy. The masses of men are sinners, and only temporal authority can provide an outward peace: "In the same way a savage wild beast is bound with chains and ropes so that it cannot bite and tear as it would normally do, even though it would like to." A society composed of such men does not have a natural order upon which a government is based, as Aristotle and St. Thomas argued. Rather, for Luther the natural socio-political state of man is Hobbesian, and the only solution is the government with its sword and law: "If this were not so, men would devour one another, seeing that the whole world is evil and that among thousands there is scarcely a single true Christian. No one could support wife and child, feed himself, and serve God. The world would be reduced to chaos."

The radical separation of the "two kingdoms" or "two governments" cannot be bridged, in Luther's mind, by the device of a holy war or crusade. As external works cannot justify, the sword cannot cause the free act of faith. In *On War Against the Turk* (1529) Luther allows for the emperor to wage war against the infidels only in order to protect his subjects. The Christian is to wage a spiritual war by prayer. In *Temporal Authority* Luther does admit the miraculous instance of Samson's fight against the Philistines where a Christian takes up the sword not for his own advantage but "to punish evil." In any case, it is the government or temporal authority, not ecclesiastical authority or the church, that is to use the sword to preserve order and punish wickedness. The converse also holds true in that the gospel cannot be used to govern the temporal world:

Hence, a man who would venture to govern an entire country or the world with the gospel would be like a shepherd who should put together in one fold wolves, lions, eagles, and sheep, and let them mingle freely with one another, saying, "Help yourselves, and be good and

8

peaceful toward one another. The fold is open, there is plenty of food. You need have no fear of dogs and clubs." The sheep would doubtless keep the peace and allow themselves to be fed and governed peacefully, but they would not live long, nor would one beast survive another.

Thus, the singular importance of temporal authority leads Luther to make his boast that "no one knew anything about temporal government" before his writing.

In the second part of *Temporal Authority* Luther delineates the major limitations on government's authority. It is restricted to "life and property and external affairs on earth," but as a divinely ordained institution it must be obeyed in these areas by all men. The soul and conscience are beyond government's jurisdiction: "The heart they cannot compel." If heresy should exist, the sword and law of the government is useless: "Here God's word must do the fighting." In the case where a ruler would suppress the Bible or other books and enforce outward compliance to religious beliefs, Luther advocates nonresistance.

The obligation to temporal authority in "external affairs" is unqualified and inconclusive. The unqualified feature is found in Luther's argument that violence against rulers for any reason is prohibited by the biblical injunction against resisting evil. The inclusive feature is seen in Luther's insistence that Christians too are as obliged as any subject. As Luther explains in *Whether Soldiers, Too, Can Be Saved*: "If worldly rulers call upon them to fight, then they ought to and must fight and be obedient, not as Christians, but as members of the state and obedient subjects. Christians therefore do not fight as individuals or for their own benefit, but as obedient servants of the authorities under whom they live." Indeed, the military profession itself is a legitimate calling for a Christian, and one must perform the tasks required by it. The extent of the obligation of the subject is due in part to Luther's view that the power of the ruler cannot affect the soul or the inner man. In *Whether Soldiers, Too, Can Be Saved* Luther writes: "If you see that the rulers think so little of their soul's salvation that they rage and do wrong, what does it matter to you if they ruin your property, body, wife, and child? They cannot hurt your soul, and they do themselves more harm than they do you because they damn their own souls and that must result in the ruin of body and property."

It is possible for political obligations to cease when conscience is impaired as with an unjust war or with the coercing of beliefs. The Scripture, conscience, and law are guides for refusing obedience, but active armed resistance by the subjects is forbidden. Luther provides a practical suggestion for solving conflicts between subjects and rulers in *Whether Soldiers, Too, Can Be Saved*: "If this king keeps neither God's law nor the law of the land, ought you to attack him, judge him, and take vengeance on him? Who commanded you to do that? Another ruler would have to come between you, hear both sides, and condemn the guilty party." In the main, the political obligations of the subject are not easily absolved.

Although it might appear that the rulers have a free hand, Luther attaches obligations also to them. In part three of *Temporal Authority* he enjoins princes to rule for the good of their people and to treat them with Christian love and service. God can, as Luther notes in *Whether Soldiers, Too, Can Be Saved*, punish tyrants with "countless ways of killing." And, the great godless multitude might wrongfully rise up and smite a tyrant, "if God so decrees." If the prince does not fulfill his obligations, then, he may suffer for it at the hand of God while on this earth as well as after death. If the subject refuses to fulfill his obligations, he suffers at the hand of the prince for disobedience, and if he actively resists the prince, he will also suffer at the hand of God for committing a sin.

The disengagement of the two kingdoms or realms results in the rulers being freed of the traditional restraints exercised by the medieval church. But for Luther the church, at once visible and invisible, is also freed from encumbrances that had corrupted Christianity. The relation between church and state consequently must change radically. The invisible church, for Luther, is simply the fellowship of believers unified in faith apart from any institutional framework. The visible church, on the other hand, includes organizations and regulations expressive of the fellowship and its witness. A logical extension of the priesthood of all believers doctrine is that church government would operate primarily by consent. In the early work, 1520, *To the Christian Nobility of the German Nation* Luther implicitly makes this argument: "Because we are all priests of equal standing, no one must push himself forward and take it upon himself, without our consent and election, to do that for which we all have equal authority." As the Reformation develops, Luther sees the need for some institutional uniformity in the church. In

1527 he and other reformers meet the problem by inviting the elector of Saxony to initiate a general "visitation of the church" in his land. The separation of the two kingdoms is preserved insofar as the elector is invited not in his capacity as prince but as a Christian, and the injunctions issued by the "visitors" are without compulsion and voluntary. The law and the sword of temporal authority are thus kept out of the spiritual realm. Luther also provides for the government to banish those who disturb the civil order by espousing religious principles which undermine the government or are simply order-disturbing. Thus, the practical requirements for organizing the visible church and the obligation of the ruler to preserve order when disturbed by false faiths do place the temporal authority in a special position. In broad terms, Luther's formula for church-state relations does forecast the later doctrine of *cuius regio, eius religio*, whereby the religion of the ruler becomes the religion of the land.

IV

All of Luther's political thought was refined in the crucible of historical events, but no one event tested his thought to the extent of the Peasants' War of 1524-25. In 1525 Luther wrote three major works on this event in which his political principles are amplified and tested: *Admonition to Peace, Against the Robbing and Murdering Hordes of Peasants*, and *An Open Letter on the Harsh Book Against the Peasants*. Peasant revolts were not uncommon in the Middle Ages, and the conditions were particularly ripe in southern Germany during the first part of the sixteenth century. There were many economic grievances prior to the Reformation itself which continued to embitter the peasants and the lower classes in the towns. In particular, the peasants were threatened by increased taxation and the imposition of Roman law and private property concepts which undermined their common use of meadows, woods, and streams. A generally deteriorating economic situation and the economic practices of ecclesiastical institutions were further burdens on the lower classes. There was also some political opposition to rulers from the towns. Luther's own thought added to the ferment. As one leading student of the Peasants' War explains: "His proclamation of the freedom of the Christian man, his criticism of the church, and the social and national notes of his great Reformation writings all fell as fertile seeds into well-prepared ground."[9] Reformers more radical than Luther, such as Andrew Karlstadt and Thomas Münzer, would appeal to the lower classes with calls for the establishing of Christian liberty on earth, the kingdom of God. In the hands of Münzer and Karlstadt the scathing attacks on medieval religious institutions became a justification for destroying monasteries and cloisters, and these theological arguments seemed just as applicable to the political hierarchy and institutions which, in their eyes, were as restrictive of Christian liberty. The Peasants' War was thus the result of an amalgam of forces ranging from simple economic injustices to millenarianism.

The first attempt by Luther to understand and ameliorate this revolutionary activity is in the *Admonition to Peace* (1525). Although Luther is sympathetic to the injustices suffered by the peasants, the tone of the work is relatively even handed in warning both peasants and rulers of God's wrath and of the possible destruction of Germany. Luther condemns the "cheating" and "robbing" of the "princes and lords, and especially you blind bishops and mad priests and monks" and places the sole blame for the rebellion on them. The peasants are told of their duty to obey authority and not to use armed rebellion in the name of the gospel. Luther bases his criticism on theological rather than economic, social, and political grounds. In the first part of the *Admonition* Luther exhorts the rulers to cease their exploitation and to moderate their position. Addressing the peasants in the second part, Luther admonishes them for destroying authority by rebelling and acting as their own judge and executor. Peace and order in the world would be destroyed by such actions, and it is contrary to the "common, divine, and natural law which even the heathen, Turks, and Jews have to keep." However just the peasants' complaints, moreover, compulsion is not compatible with Christian doctrine. The peasants are especially guilty, in Luther's mind, of the millenarian sin of identifying their cause with the gospel and Christ. In other words, the two kingdoms have been bridged by the peasants. The true Christian, says Luther, "would stop threatening and resisting with fist and sword" but would "endure and suffer wrong and . . . pray to God in every need." The kingdom of God is spiritual and not dependent

---

[9] Hubert Kirchner, *Luther and the Peasants' War*, trans. Darrell Jodock (Philadelphia: Fortress Press, 1972), p. 6.

upon the structure of a political system. Even a "slave can be a Christian, and have Christian freedom." The freedom and equality of the kingdom of God are not for this worldly kingdom, which "cannot exist without an inequality of persons, some being free, some imprisoned, some lords, some subjects." Even if the ruler should not "tolerate the pastor whom they chose and support," the subjects are not justified to take up arms but must simply "flee to another city." The two kingdoms must be kept separate in practice as well as theory. He concludes the work by calling for arbitration so that "a solution of this dispute through human laws and agreements, if not through Christian means" can be obtained.

The *Admonition to Peace* was published too late to affect the general insurrection. Luther next wrote *Against the Robbing and Murdering Hordes of Peasants*. Originally, this work was published with a new edition of the *Admonition* and with the title of *Against the Robbing and Murdering Hordes of the* Other *Peasants*. Apparently, Luther wished to make clear that the second tract was aimed at only the actual fighting peasants. All other editions omitted "Other," and the qualification was lost to Luther's contemporaries.[10] In this work Luther is convinced that rebellion and anarchy are at hand and that "the destruction of the world is to be expected every hour." Luther reiterates the three major sins of the rebelling peasants. First, they have broken Christ's commandments by violating their "oath of obedience" to the temporal authority. Second, they have started a rebellion and caused all the horrors of war, "a land filled with murder and bloodshed; it makes widows and orphans, and turns everything upside down, like the worst disaster." Third, they compel belief and blaspheme God by acting in the name of the gospel. On all these grounds the peasants merit death. Luther instructs all princes, as God's ministers, to do their duty and punish the rebels: "If he is able to punish and does not do it—even though he would have had to kill someone or shed blood—he becomes guilty of all the murder and evil that these people commit." In his most shocking statement, Luther exhorts "everyone who can, smite, slay, and stab, secretly or openly, remembering that nothing can be more poisonous, hurtful, or devilish than a rebel." Luther also assures the lords that if one should lose his life in fighting the rebels, he would be a martyr with a "blessed death."

---

10 Ibid., p. 11.

The harshness of the nobles' treatment of the defeated peasants and the harshness of Luther's tract against the peasants led friends and foes alike to criticize Luther. In his own defense Luther published *An Open Letter on the Harsh Book Against the Peasants*. He does not recant, and, indeed, he argues that those who are now sympathetic for the rebels are themselves "rebels at heart." Luther does note that the tract against the peasants was aimed at actual rebels who were "raging, smiting, robbing, burning, and plundering." In the main, Luther simply reminds the reader that he was following the incontestable words of God. There are two kingdoms, and the Christian's duty is to suffer and pray in this world; it is not to take the sword against temporal authority. The kingdom of this world is one of "wrath and severity," and it should be kept separate from the kingdom of God. The blasphemous peasants did not maintain the separation and they must be punished. Whereas a murderer attacks only an individual, a rebel is particularly odious because he destroys temporal authority itself. The civil order must be protected even under the Turks: "Even if I served a Turk and saw my Lord in danger, I would forget my spiritual office and stab and hew as long as my heart beat." Rebellion, Luther continues, "is a crime that deserves neither a court trial nor mercy." On the other hand, the princes are abusing their office by their revenge on the defeated peasants. The rulers should repent of their blood lust and show mercy, but Luther himself accepts no responsibility for instructing rulers to be harsh and warns of God's wrath on their eternal souls.

Did the crucible of the Peasants' War seriously change Luther's political principles? There seems little evidence of a change. The doctrine of the two kingdoms is firmly adhered to throughout the insurrection. The divinely ordained status of temporal authority is constantly cited in condemning the act of rebellion. The obligations of the subjects are not diminished even when a pastor is not tolerated by a ruler. The Christian subject is continuously counseled to suffer, pray, and practice nonresistance. Luther throughout is not simply opposed to peasants while favoring rulers. He is constantly opposed to rebellion and offensive warfare: he opposed the rebellion of knights in the Sickingen War of 1522, he opposed the Peasants' War of 1525, and he opposed an offensive crusade against the Turks in 1529.

Luther's reputation was harmed by the Peasants' War and by

his various tracts on it. Although there is evidence that the spontaneous growth of the Reformation continued in north Germany, its appeal in south Germany to the lower classes and the peasantry was severely reduced.[11] If regrettable for these reasons, Luther's response to the war nevertheless was consistent with the theological mode through which he understood historical events. There were biblical arguments which demanded, for example, obedience to temporal authority, and there were similar arguments for the use of the sword against the rebels. The two kingdoms doctrine of Luther cannot be reconciled with the millenarianism of some peasant leaders. Lastly, the Bible for Luther clearly could countenance only nonresistance, never the sword. When pressed by the Peasants' War, Luther's theological principles left him little choice but to translate the historical events of the insurrection into his antithetical theological categories: divinely ordained temporal authority or the holocaust of disorder and the last days, the kingdom of God with love and mercy or the kingdom of the world with the sword and repression, the radical separation of the two kingdoms or the heresy of millenarianism. Luther's theological understanding of the Peasants' War may indeed be correct. Certainly it was Luther's intent to provide a spiritual and theological examination of political millenarianism. But antithetical categories do not easily lend themselves to realistic reforms or to moderate advice on the economic, social, and political level.

Luther again discusses resistance, rebellion, and the duty to obey in his 1531 work, *Dr. Martin Luther's Warning to His Dear German People.* The context for this discussion is quite different from that in the Peasants' War. After the Diet of Augsburg (1530) Emperor Charles V proclaimed that the error of the Protestants had been refuted and that a six-month period was provided for removing the heresy from Germany. It was possible that the emperor would use force to erase the Reformation. The limits on the obligations of the subjects and thus the possibility of justified disobedience was recognized by Luther in various writings prior to 1531. But in the *Warning* Luther appears to go further and to justify armed resistance rather than nonresistance.

---

[11] Franz Lau, "Did Popular Reformation Really Stop With the Peasants' Defeat?", *Reformation and Authority: The Meaning of the Peasants' Revolt,* ed. Kyle C. Sessions (Lexington, Mass.: D. C. Heath, 1968), pp. 94–101. This book provides an excellent survey of various interpretations of the Peasants' War.

Luther finds it very difficult to examine the political reality of an imperial war directed at the Reformation: "We are now speaking as in a dream, as if there were no God. . . ." Yet, Luther proceeds, if war in fact should come, the Protestants are innocent of it because peace and nonresistance have always been preached by them. The onus for war must be on the papists. In this eventuality, Luther maintains that he will neither write against it nor "reprove those who defend themselves against the murderous and bloodthirsty papists, nor let anyone else rebuke them as being seditious, but I will accept their action and let it pass as self-defense." This cautious approval of self-defense is immediately surrounded with several qualifications. First, as a Christian theologian Luther does not "wish to incite or spur anyone on to such self-defense, or to justify it, for that is not my office." Second, Luther argues that self-defense can be justified by the "law and the Jurists." Third, active self-defense would not be a rebellion in the precise sense because the Protestants do keep the peace and would not overthrow authority while the papists refuse to keep the peace and would start the war. When Luther develops his position, he does not entirely shift the responsibility of advice to the jurists:

> If the emperor should issue a call to arms against us on behalf of the pope or because of our teaching . . . no one should lend himself to it or obey the emperor in this event. All may rest assured that God has strictly forbidden compliance with such a command of the emperor. Whoever does obey him can be certain that he is disobedient to God and will lose both body and soul eternally in the war. For in this case the emperor would not only act in contravention of God and divine law but also in violation of his own imperial law, vow, duty, seal and edicts.

Luther then lists for the reader three "strong reasons" in support of this advice: "you . . . vowed in baptism to preserve the gospel of Christ and not to persecute it or oppose it"; "you should . . . be deterred from fighting solely by the knowledge that by such fighting you are taking upon yourself a part of the guilt before God of all the abominations which have been committed and will yet be committed by the whole papacy"; "you must refuse obedience . . . otherwise . . . you would also lend a hand in overthrowing and exterminating all the good which the dear gospel has again restored and established."

16

Some interpreters of Luther have argued that his "advice" and "strong reasons" are only grounds for nonresistance and are not grounds for active self-defense.[12] The "advice," strictly speaking, is to disobey the emperor, and the reasons are given to justify not fighting in the emperor's war. Luther does not give the positive advice to fight in self-defense, although that meaning may easily be inferred by the reader. Other scholars have contended that in the *Warning* Luther has made a major change in his political thought by justifying active self-defense:

> Insurrection, to be sure, is still forbidden to the Christian; but defensive action in protection of the gospel—even if military means be used, and even if these be directed against the emperor—is not to be counted as insurrection. The use of force in such circumstances may be justified, as in the case of a "just war" according to the classic doctrine, if the end is just, the means appropriate, and if all peaceful means of settlement have failed.[13]

It could be contended that Luther consistently gives reasons derived from the gospel for nonresistance, and, in this particular case, he also accepts the justification for active self-defense as espoused by the law and the jurists. There would still be the difficulty of reconciling Luther's acceptance of the legal justification for active self-defense with his absolute prohibition on using violence against rulers found in other writings. Thus, there does appear to be a change in his political thought.

V

Luther wrote on a wide range of social and political topics, from educational reform to usury. This selection from his writings provides only an introduction to a few major themes in his political thought—the nature of temporal authority, political obligation and its limits, church-state relations, and political resistance. After reading these selections, a reader should appreciate at least the honest conviction and candor with which Luther wrote. The careful reader

---

[12] Allen, *History of Political Thought*, pp. 27–28; Mulford Q. Sibley, *Political Ideas and Ideologies: A History of Political Thought* (New York: Harper and Row, 1960), p. 317. For a classic statement of the position that nonresistance is an integral part of Luther's political thought, see Niebuhr, *Nature and Destiny of Man*, 2:185–95.

[13] Frank Sherman, "Introduction," *Luther's Works*, vol. 47, *The Christian in Society*, IV, trans. Martin H. Bertram (Philadelphia: Fortress Press, 1971), p. 7; V. H. H. Green, *Luther and the Reformation* (London: University Paperback, 1969), pp. 176–77; Grimm, *The Reformation Era*, p. 571.

could also reach some conclusions about the substance and merit of his political thought. In this regard, it would certainly be possible to stress the ambiguities in Luther's thought. One contemporary political thinker writes:

> Luther . . . vehemently rejected any hierarchical distinctions among Christian believers; yet he assumed that a social hierarchy was natural and necessary. He eloquently defended the sanctity of the individual conscience; yet he unhesitatingly accepted the institutions of serfdom. He admitted that some of the grievances of the peasants were justified, but counseled the peasant against attaching much value to material concerns. He was willing to raise fundamental questions about every form of religious authority, but towards political institutions he was quite unsceptical, even when he doubted the morals and motives of rulers. His thought represented a striking combination of revolt and passivity.[14]

While there is clearly some truth in this assessment, a fairer and more complete judgment requires a recognition of the other elements in Luther's political thought which have enduring significance. In particular, there are three areas in political thought where Luther has made lasting contributions.

First, Luther knew that to understand the state or temporal authority one must recognize the reality of power and one must see that power's chief justification is found in securing order and peace. This concern for understanding power and its justification places Luther in that remarkable group of political thinkers who are the precursors of modern political thought: Machiavelli (1460-1527), Luther (1483-1546), Bodin (1530-1596), and Hobbes (1588-1679). Within the historical context of the rising nations of Italy, Germany, France, and England these formative thinkers perceived the reality of power, and they explained and justified temporal authority or the state with arguments which distinguished them from the medieval and classical ages. In the main, they saw politics as the realm of force, selfishness, and domination, but they also held that the state or temporal authority could provide peace and order. It was necessary for them to explain and understand power, for it appeared to have a pattern and development which could not be understood by simply discussing religious and philosophic sources of authority. Each of these political thinkers saw this task as a new

---

[14] Sheldon S. Wolin, *Politics and Vision: Continuity and Innovation in Western Political Thought* (Boston: Little, Brown, 1960), p. 164.

one, and, as with Luther, each made the claim that he was an originator.

Luther alone relied solely upon theological language to explain and justify temporal authority. Through the doctrine of the two kingdoms Luther is able to de-divinize politics and to emphasize the separateness and reality of power. As a consequence, Luther places the *raison d'etre* for the state in its ability and power to provide order, continuity, and permanence rather than in its relation to the kingdom of God. Although Luther does not distinguish clearly among the concepts power, force, violence, legitimacy, sovereignty, and authority—nor did he attempt to do so as did Bodin or Hobbes —yet he was aware that the ability and power of any state to function and attain its proper ends could not be explained as mere force. Thus, the *raison d'etre* or justification of temporal authority provided by Luther applied to all states, Roman Catholic, Protestant, and Turkish, because all exercise power and seek order.

While Luther is aware of the autonomy of temporal authority and the reality of power, the doctrine of the two kingdoms indicates that he does not worship power. Besides accentuating the autonomy of secular power, the doctrine also serves to emphasize the limitations of power: it could not enter the realm of the soul and spiritual freedom. Moreover, Luther's vivid and candid description of the kingdom of the world directs ones attention away from this world to the kingdom of God. Lastly, for Luther political turmoil and the worship of power are less likely to distract people from the worship of God if they understand temporal authority and its limited ends of social peace and order.

A second area where Luther made a significant contribution is in understanding political millenarianism. If Hobbes, Bobin, and Machiavelli show greater analytic clarity than Luther in defining such concepts as legitimacy, sovereignty, and power, Luther alone identified political millenarian movements and developed a critique of them. Luther saw two key attributes which identify such movements: their appeal is to immanentize the kingdom of God and thus abolish the distinction between the two kingdoms, and they use power to compel the conscience or the inner man in order to serve spiritual perfection. The movement led by Thomas Münzer was diagnosed by Luther as a clear case of this phenomenon. Luther also saw several attempts to create millenarian movements such as the call for a holy war against the Turks. One can cull from Luther's writings two major arguments used in refutation of such movements. First, man's nature is such that he cannot achieve perfection even if he should be a true Christian. Second, the goal of perfection does not belong to the political realm. To achieve perfection, grace and love are the required means, not the power used by the kingdom of this world. In sum, the end of perfection is beyond the power of man, for the kingdom of God is entered by faith through God's grace. Here again Luther's contribution is made in theological language, which may seem archaic and awkward to modern ears; nevertheless, one would be hard pressed to find arguments more concise and cogent for identifying and refuting political millenarianism.

A third area where Luther's political thought contains significant and relevant insights is in the relation between politics and ideology. In many ways, Luther appears to illustrate the relation between politics and ideology sometimes found in contemporary political life. Certainly he often wrote expressly for a mass audience, as would be required of any leader today who wished to create a new body politic. He also wrote in the style of a public leader, that is, to provide guidance in the shaping of the course of events and to exhort his public with slogans and formulas easily grasped by a mass audience. All of this appears quite similar to the style and substance of political speeches used by many a founder of a modern political movement or of a state. Indeed, it is sometimes argued that part of Luther's significance is that he was a creator of a mass movement. As such, Luther's thought shows those features which are associated with modern ideological politics: political ideas become levers of action and there is a unity of theory and practice. Implicit in this concern for political action is a preoccupation with consequences rather than with intrinsic content as in the case for political philosophy. Thus, some thinkers have judged Luther's political thought to be "ominously modern."[15]

On the other hand, Luther's thought as a whole can be interpreted to provide little support for ideological thinking and politics. His theological doctrines accentuate the personal religious freedom of the Christian and the sanctity of the individual, and such themes would not be possible without also holding that the autonomous

---

[15] Ibid., p. 194.

individual can understand by himself and thus be changed. If the individual could be molded and changed by society and by the slogans of a belief system or ideology, then there could not be the truly personal freedom and individual conscience claimed by Luther. Through such theological concepts as conscience and freedom, Luther is supporting the view that autonomous thought or ideas themselves can change man without recourse to political action. Likewise, such political tenets as the limiting of power's efficacy and jurisdiction to the outer man, and the tenets contained in his vehement attacks on political millenarianism, all would scarcely allow Luther to advocate a position similar to that unity of theory and practice which is fundamental to ideological thinking. Finally, Luther's own practice as a Reformation leader provides little evidence that he was a practitioner of ideological politics. He repeatedly insisted that the gospel would stand by itself without political support, and he conducted his Reformation leadership primarily through ideas themselves rather than through political maneuvers. One can conclude that Luther's thought and leadership support the separation of theory and practice, the supremacy of political philosophy over ideology, and the position that autonomous thought or ideas can shape the course of history.

SELECTED BIBLIOGRAPHY

A sizable portion of Luther's vast writings are now available in the new American Edition of *Luther's Works* (Philadelphia: Fortress, and St. Louis: Concordia, 1955–   ), the edition from which the texts in this book have been excerpted and which is hereinafter referred to as *LW*.

Biographies of Luther

Bainton, Roland H. *Here I Stand: A Life of Martin Luther.* New York: New American Library, 1962.

Boehmer, Heinrich. *Road to Reformation.* Translated by John W. Doberstein and Theodore G. Tappert. New York: Meridian, 1957.

Green, V. H. H. *Luther and the Reformation.* London: University Paperback, 1969.

Lau, Franz. *Luther.* Translated by Robert H. Fischer. Philadelphia: Westminster Press, 1962. This book provides an excellent introduction to Luther and has an annotated bibliography.

Ritter, Gerhard. *Luther: His Life and Work.* Translated by John Riches. New York: Harper and Row, 1963.

Rupp, Gordon. *Luther's Progress to the Diet of Worms.* Chicago: Wilcox and Follett, 1951.

Schwiebert, Ernest G. *Luther and his Times: The Reformation from a new Perspective.* St. Louis: Concordia Publishing House, 1950.

Thiel, Rudolf. *Luther.* Translated by Gustav K. Wiencke. Philadelphia: Muhlenberg Press, 1955.

Thulin, Oskar. *A Life of Luther Told in Pictures and Narrative by the Reformer and His Contemporaries.* Translated by Martin O. Dietrich. Philadelphia: Fortress Press, 1966.

General Histories of the Reformation

Bainton, Roland H. *The Reformation of the Sixteenth Century.* Boston: Beacon Press, 1956.

Elton, G. R., ed. *The New Cambridge Modern History.* Vol. 2: *The Reformation 1520–1559.* Cambridge: Cambridge University Press, 1958.

Grimm, Harold J. *The Reformation Era, 1500–1650.* New York: Macmillan, 1954.

Holl, Karl. *The Cultural Significance of the Reformation.* Introduction by Wilhelm Pauck. New York: Meridian, 1959.

Mosse, George L. *The Reformation.* New York: Holt, Rinehart and Winston, 1963.

Pauck, Wilhelm. *The Heritage of the Reformation.* Glencoe, Ill.: Free Press, 1961.

Smith, Preserved. *The Age of the Reformation.* New York: Holt, 1936.

Theology and Political Thought

Althaus, Paul. *The Theology of Martin Luther.* Translated by Robert C. Schultz. Philadelphia: Fortress Press, 1966.

————. *The Ethics of Martin Luther.* Philadelphia: Fortress Press, 1972.

Bornkamm, Heinrich. *Luther's Doctrines of the Two Kingdoms.* Translated by Karl H. Hertz. Philadelphia: Fortress Press, 1966.

Cranz, F. Edward. *An Essay on the Development of Luther's Thought on Justice, Law, and Society.* Cambridge: Harvard University Press, 1964.

Davies, R. E. *The Problem of Authority in the Continental Reformers.* London: Epworth Press, 1946.

Ebeling, Gerhard. *Luther: An Introduction to His Thought.* Translated by R. A. Wilson. Philadelphia: Fortress Press, 1970.

Forell, George W. *Faith Active in Love: An Investigation of the Principles Underlying Luther's Social Ethics.* New York: American Press, 1954.

Kirchner, Hubert. *Luther and the Peasants' War.* Translated by Darrell Jodock. Philadelphia: Fortress Press, 1972.

Mueller, William A. *Church and State in Luther and Calvin: A Comparative Study.* Nashville: Broadmen Press, 1954.

Rupp, E. Gordon. *The Righteousness of God.* Naperville, Ill.: Allenson, 1953.

Sessions, Kyle C., ed. *Reformation and Authority: The Meaning of the Peasants' Revolt.* Lexington, Mass.: D. C. Heath, 1968. This book contains an excellent annotated bibliography.

Thielicke, Helmut. *Theological Ethics, Volume 2: Politics.* Edited by William H. Lazareth. Philadelphia: Fortress Press, 1969.

Watson, Philip S. *Let God be God! An Interpretation of the Theology of Luther.* Philadelphia: Fortress Press, 1965.

Wingren, Gustaf. *Luther on Vocation.* Philadelphia: Fortress Press, 1957.

Wolin, Sheldon S. *Politics and Vision: Continuity and Innovation in Western Political Thought.* Boston: Little, Brown, 1960. Especially chapters 5 and 6.

of all, was "born of woman, born under the law" [Gal. 4:4], and therefore was at the same time a free man and a servant, "in the form of God" and "of a servant" [Phil. 2:6-7].

Let us start, however, with something more remote from our subject, but more obvious. Man has a twofold nature, a spiritual and a bodily one. According to the spiritual nature, which men refer to as the soul, he is called a spiritual, inner, or new man. According to the bodily nature, which men refer to as flesh, he is called a carnal, outward, or old man, of whom the Apostle writes in II Cor. 4 [:16], "Though our outer nature is wasting away, our inner nature is being renewed every day." Because of this diversity of nature the Scriptures assert contradictory things concerning the same man, since these two men in the same man contradict each other, "for the desires of the flesh are against the Spirit, and the desires of the Spirit are against the flesh," according to Gal. 5 [:17].

First, let us consider the inner man to see how a righteous, free, and pious Christian, that is, a spiritual, new, and inner man, becomes what he is. It is evident that no external thing has any influence in producing Christian righteousness or freedom, or in producing unrighteousness or servitude. A simple argument will furnish the proof of this statement. What can it profit the soul if the body is well, free, and active, and eats, drinks, and does as it pleases? For in these respects even the most godless slaves of vice may prosper. On the other hand, how will poor health or imprisonment or hunger or thirst or any other external misfortune harm the soul? Even the most godly men, and those who are free because of clear consciences, are afflicted with these things. None of these things touch either the freedom or the servitude of the soul. It does not help the soul if the body is adorned with the sacred robes of priests or dwells in sacred places or is occupied with sacred duties or prays, fasts, abstains from certain kinds of food, or does any work that can be done by the body and in the body. The righteousness and the freedom of the soul require something far different since the things which have been mentioned could be done by any wicked person. Such works produce nothing but hypocrites. On the other hand, it will not harm the soul if the body is clothed in secular dress, dwells in unconsecrated places, eats and drinks as others do, does not pray aloud, and neglects to do all the above-mentioned things which hypocrites can do.

Furthermore, to put aside all kinds of works, even contemplation, meditation, and all that the soul can do, does not help. One thing, and only one thing, is necessary for Christian life, righteousness, and freedom. That one thing is the most holy Word of God, the gospel of Christ, as Christ says, John 11 [:25], "I am the resurrection and the life; he who believes in me, though he die, yet shall he live"; and John 8 [:36], "So if the Son makes you free, you will be free indeed"; and Matt. 4 [:4], "Man shall not live by bread alone, but by every word that proceeds from the mouth of God." Let us then consider it certain and firmly established that the soul can do without anything except the Word of God and that where the Word of God is missing there is no help at all for the soul. If it has the Word of God it is rich and lacks nothing since it is the Word of life, truth, light, peace, righteousness, salvation, joy, liberty, wisdom, power, grace, glory, and of every incalculable blessing. This is why the prophet in the entire Psalm [119] and in many other places yearns and sighs for the Word of God and uses so many names to describe it.

On the other hand, there is no more terrible disaster with which the wrath of God can afflict men than a famine of the hearing of his Word, as he says in Amos [8:11]. Likewise there is no greater mercy than when he sends forth his Word, as we read in Psalm 107 [:20]: "He sent forth his word, and healed them, and delivered them from destruction." Nor was Christ sent into the world for any other ministry except that of the Word. Moreover, the entire spiritual estate—all the apostles, bishops, and priests— has been called and instituted only for the ministry of the Word.

You may ask, "What then is the Word of God, and how shall it be used, since there are so many words of God?" I answer: The Apostle explains this in Romans 1. The Word is the gospel of God concerning his Son, who was made flesh, suffered, rose from the dead, and was glorified through the Spirit who sanctifies. To preach Christ means to feed the soul, make it righteous, set it free, and save it, provided it believes the preaching. Faith alone is the saving and efficacious use of the Word of God, according to Rom. 10 [:9]: "If you confess with your lips that Jesus is Lord and believe in your heart that God raised him from the dead, you will be saved." Furthermore, "Christ is the end of the law, that every one who has faith may be justified" [Rom. 10:4]. Again, in Rom. 1 [:17], "He who through faith is righteous shall live." The Word of God cannot be received and cherished by any works whatever but only by faith. Therefore it is clear that, as the soul needs only the Word of God for its life and righteousness, so it is justified by faith alone and not any works; for if it could be justified by anything else, it would not need the Word, and consequently it would not need faith.

This faith cannot exist in connection with works—that is to say, if you at the same time claim to be justified by works, whatever their character—for that would be the same as "limping with two different opinions" [I Kings 18:21], as worshiping Baal and kissing one's own hand [Job 31:27-28], which, as Job says, is a very great iniquity. Therefore the moment you begin to have faith you learn that all things in you are altogether blameworthy, sinful, and damnable, as the Apostle says in Rom. 3 [:23], "Since all have sinned and fall short of the glory of God," and, "None is righteous, no, not one; . . . all have turned aside, together they have gone wrong" (Rom. 3:10-12). When you have learned this you will know that you need Christ, who suffered and rose again for you so that, if you believe in him, you may through this faith become a new man in so far as your sins are forgiven and you are justified by the merits of another, namely, of Christ alone.

Since, therefore, this faith can rule only in the inner man, as Rom. 10 [:10] says, "For man believes with his heart and so is justified," and since faith alone justifies, it is clear that the inner man cannot be justified, freed, or saved by any outer work or action at all, and that these works, whatever their character, have nothing to do with this inner man. On the other hand, only ungodliness and unbelief of heart, and no outer work, make him guilty and a damnable servant of sin. Wherefore it ought to be the first concern of every Christian to lay aside all confidence in works and increasingly to strengthen faith alone and through faith to grow in the knowledge, not of works, but of Christ Jesus, who suffered and rose for him, as Peter teaches in the last chapter of his first Epistle (I Pet. 5:10). No other work makes a Christian. Thus when the Jews asked Christ, as related in John 6 [:28], what they must do "to be doing the work of God," he brushed aside the multitude of works which he saw they did in great profusion and suggested one work, saying, "This is the work of God, that you believe in him whom he has sent" [John 6:29]; "for on him has God the Father set his seal" [John 6:27].

Therefore true faith in Christ is a treasure beyond comparison which brings with it complete salvation and saves man from every evil, as Christ says in the last chapter of Mark [16:16]: "He who believes and is baptized will be saved; but he who does not believe will be condemned." Isaiah contemplated this treasure and foretold it in chapter 10: "The Lord will make a small and consuming word upon the land, and it will overflow with righteousness" [Cf. Isa. 10:22]. This is as though he said, "Faith, which is a small and perfect fulfilment of the law, will fill believers with so great a righteousness that they will need nothing more to become righteous." So Paul says, Rom. 10 [:10], "For man believes with his heart and so is justified."

Should you ask how it happens that faith alone justifies and offers us such a treasure of great benefits without works in view of the fact that so many works, ceremonies, and laws are prescribed in the Scriptures, I answer: First of all, remember what has been said, namely, that faith alone, without works, justifies, frees, and saves; we shall make this clearer later on. Here we must point out that the entire Scripture of God is divided into two parts: commandments and promises. Although the commandments teach things that are good, the things taught are not done as soon as they are taught, for the commandments show us what we ought to do but do not give us the power to do it. They are intended to teach man to know himself, that through them he may recognize his inability to do good and may despair of his own ability. That is why they are called the Old Testament and constitute the Old Testament. For example, the commandment, "You shall not covet" [Exod. 20:17], is a command which proves us all to be sinners, for no one can avoid coveting no matter how much he may struggle against it. Therefore, in order not to covet and to fulfil the commandment, a man is compelled to despair of himself, to seek the help which he does not find in himself elsewhere and from someone else, as stated in Hosea [13:9]: "Destruction is your own, O Israel: your help is only in me." As we fare with respect to one commandment, so we fare with all, for it is equally impossible for us to keep any one of them.

Now when a man has learned through the commandments to recognize his helplessness and is distressed about how he might satisfy the law—since the law must be fulfilled so that not a jot or tittle shall be lost, otherwise man will be condemned without hope—then, being truly humbled and reduced to nothing in his own eyes, he finds in himself nothing whereby he may be justified and saved. Here the second part of Scripture comes to our aid, namely, the promises of God which declare the glory of God, saying, "If you wish to fulfil the law and not covet, as the law demands, come, believe in Christ in whom grace, righteousness, peace, liberty, and all things are promised you. If you believe, you shall have all things; if you do not believe, you shall lack all things." That which is impossible for you to accomplish by trying to fulfil all the works of the law—many and useless as they all are—you will accomplish quickly and easily through faith. God our Father has made all things depend on faith so that whoever has faith will have everything, and whoever does not have faith will have nothing. "For God has consigned all men to disobedience, that he may have mercy upon all," as it is stated in Rom. 11 [:32]. Thus the promises of God give what the commandments of God demand and fulfil what the law prescribes so that all things may be God's alone, both the commandments and the fulfilling of the commandments. He alone commands, he alone fulfils. Therefore the promises of God belong to the New Testament. Indeed, they are the New Testament.

Since these promises of God are holy, true, righteous, free, and peaceful words, full of goodness, the soul which clings to them with a firm faith will be so closely united with them and altogether absorbed by them that it not only will share in all their power but will be saturated and intoxicated by them. If a touch of Christ healed, how much more will this most tender spiritual touch, this absorbing of the Word, communicate to the soul all things that belong to the Word. This, then, is how through faith alone without works the soul is justified by the Word of God, sanctified, made true, peaceful, and free, filled with every blessing and truly made a child of God, as John 1 [:12] says: "But to all who . . . believed in his name, he gave power to become children of God."

From what has been said it is easy to see from what source faith derives such great power and why a good work or all good works together cannot equal it. No good work can rely upon the Word of God or live in the soul, for faith alone and the Word of God rule in the soul. Just as the heated iron glows like fire because of the union of fire with it, so the Word imparts its qualities to the soul. It is clear, then, that a Christian has all that he needs in faith and needs no works to justify him; and if he has no need of works, he has no need of the law; and if he has no need of the law, surely he is free from the law. It is true that "the law is not laid down for the just" [I Tim. 1:9]. This is that Christian liberty, our faith, which does not induce us to live in idleness or wickedness but makes the law and works unnecessary for any man's righteousness and salvation.

* * *

That we may examine more profoundly that grace which our inner man has in Christ, we must realize that in the Old Testament God consecrated to himself all the first-born males. The birthright was highly prized for it involved a twofold honor, that of priesthood and that of kingship.

* * *

The nature of this priesthood and kingship is something like this: First, with respect to the kingship, every Christian is by faith so exalted above all things that, by virtue of a spiritual power, he is lord of all things without exception, so that nothing can do him any harm. As a matter of fact, all things are made subject to him and are compelled to serve him in obtaining salvation. Accordingly Paul says in Rom. 8 [:28], "All things work together for good for the elect," and in I Cor. 3 [:21-23], "All things are yours whether ... life or death or the present or the future, all are yours; and you are Christ's. . . ." This is not to say that every Christian is placed over all things to have and control them by physical power—a madness with which some churchmen are afflicted—for such power belongs to kings, princes, and other men on earth. Our ordinary experience in life shows us that we are subjected to all, suffer many things, and even die. As a matter of fact, the more Christian a man is, the more evils, sufferings, and deaths he must endure, as we see in Christ the first-born prince himself, and in all his brethren, the saints. The power of which we speak is spirtual. It rules in the midst of enemies and is powerful in the midst of oppression. This means nothing else than that "power is made perfect in weakness" [II Cor. 12:9] and that in all things I can find profit toward salvation [Rom. 8:28], so that the cross and death itself are compelled to serve me and to work together with me for my salvation. This is a splendid privilege and hard to attain, a truly omnipotent power, a spiritual dominion in which there is nothing so good and nothing so evil but that it shall work together for good to me, if only I believe. Yes, since faith alone suffices for salvation, I need nothing except faith exercising the power and dominion of its own liberty. Lo, this is the inestimable power and liberty of Christians.

Not only are we the freest of kings, we are also priests forever, which is far more excellent than being kings, for as priests we are worthy to appear before God to pray for others and to teach one another divine things. These are the functions of priests, and they cannot be granted to any unbeliever. Thus Christ has made it possible for us, provided we believe in him, to be not only his brethren, co-heirs, and fellow-kings, but also his fellow-priests. Therefore we may boldly come into the presence of God in the spirit of faith [Heb. 10:19, 22] and cry "Abba, Father!" pray for one another, and do all things which we see done and foreshadowed in the outer and visible works of priests.

* * *

From this anyone can clearly see how a Christian is free from all things and over all things so that he needs no works to make him righteous and save him, since faith alone abundantly confers all these things. Should he grow so foolish, however, as to presume to become righteous, free, saved, and a Christian by means of some good work, he would instantly lose faith and all its benefits, a foolishness aptly illustrated in the fable of the dog who runs along a stream with a piece of meat in his mouth and, deceived by the reflection of the meat in the water, opens his mouth to snap at it and so loses both the meat and the reflection.

You will ask, "If all who are in the church are priests, how do these whom we now call priests differ from laymen?" I answer: Injustice is done those words "priest," "cleric," "spiritual," "ecclesiastic," when they are transferred from all Christians to those few who are now by a mischievous usage called "ecclesiastics." Holy Scripture makes no distinction between them, although it gives the name "ministers," "servants," "stewards" to those who are now proudly called popes, bishops, and lords and who should according to the ministry of the Word serve others and teach them the faith of Christ and the freedom of believers. Although we are all equally priests, we cannot all publicly minister and teach. We ought not do so even if we could. Paul writes accordingly in I Cor. 4 [1],

"This is how one should regard us, as servants of Christ and stewards of the mysteries of God."

* * *

Let this suffice concerning the inner man, his liberty, and the source of his liberty, the righteousness of faith. He needs neither laws nor good works but, on the contrary, is injured by them if he believes that he is justified by them.

Now let us turn to the second part, the outer man. Here we shall answer all those who, offended by the word "faith" and by all that has been said, now ask, "If faith does all things and is alone sufficient unto righteousness, why then are good works commanded? We will take our ease and do no works and be content with faith." I answer: not so, you wicked men, not so. That would indeed be proper if we were wholly inner and perfectly spiritual men. But such we shall be only at the last day, the day of the resurrection of the dead. As long as we live in the flesh we only begin to make some progress in that which shall be perfected in the future life. For this reason the Apostle in Rom. 8 [:23] calls all that we attain in this life "the first fruits of the Spirit" because we shall indeed receive the greater portion, even the fulness of the Spirit, in the future. This is the place to assert that which was said above, namely, that a Christian is the servant of all and made subject to all. Insofar as he is free he does no works, but insofar as he is a servant he does all kinds of works. How this is possible we shall see.

Although, as I have said, a man is abundantly and sufficiently justified by faith inwardly, in his spirit, and so has all that he needs, except insofar as this faith and these riches must grow from day to day even to the future life; yet he remains in this mortal life on earth. In this life he must control his own body and have dealings with men. Here the works begin; here a man cannot enjoy leisure; here he must indeed take care to discipline his body by fastings, watchings, labors, and other reasonable discipline and to subject it to the Spirit so that it will obey and conform to the inner man and faith and not revolt against faith and hinder the inner man, as it is the nature of the body to do if it is not held in check. The inner man, who by faith is created in the image of God, is both joyful and happy because of Christ in whom so many benefits are conferred upon him; and therefore it is his one occupation to serve God joyfully and without thought of gain, in love that is not constrained.

* * *

In order to make that which we have said more easily understood, we shall explain by analogies. We should think of the works of a Christian who is justified and saved by faith because of the pure and free mercy of God, just as we would think of the works which Adam and Eve did in Paradise, and all their children would have done if they had not sinned. We read in Gen. 2 [:15] that "The Lord God took the man and put him in the garden of Eden to till it and keep it." Now Adam was created righteous and upright and without sin by God so that he had no need of being justified and made upright through his tilling and keeping the garden; but, that he might not be idle, the Lord gave him a task to do, to cultivate and protect the garden. This task would truly have been the freest of works, done only to please God and not to obtain righteousness, which Adam already had in full measure and which would have been the birthright of us all.

* * *

From this it is easy to know how far good works are to be rejected or not, and by what standard all the teachings of men concerning works are to be interpreted. If works are sought after as a means to righteousness, are burdened with this perverse leviathan, and are done under the false impression that through them one is justified, they are made necessary and freedom and faith are destroyed; and this addition to them makes them no longer good but truly damnable works. They are not free, and they blaspheme the grace of God since to justify and to save by faith belongs to the grace of God alone. What the works have no power to do they nevertheless—by a godless presumption through this folly of ours—pretend to do and thus violently force themselves into the office and glory of grace. We do not, therefore, reject good works; on the contrary, we cherish and teach them as much as possible. We do not condemn them for their own sake but on account of this godless addition to them and the perverse idea that righteousness is to be sought through them; for that makes them appear good outwardly, when in truth they are not good. They deceive men and lead them to deceive one another like ravening wolves in sheep's clothing [Matt. 7:15].

* * *

Of the same nature are the precepts which Paul gives in Rom. 13 [:1-7], namely, that Christians should be subject to the governing authorities and be ready to do every good work, not that they shall in this way be justified, since they already are righteous through faith, but that in the liberty of the Spirit they shall by so doing serve others and the authorities themselves and obey their will freely and out of love. The works of all colleges, * monasteries, and priests should be of this nature. Each one should do the works of his profession and station, not that by them he may strive after righteousness, but that through them he may keep his body under control, be an example to others who also need to keep their bodies under control, and finally that by such works he may submit his will to that of others in the freedom of love. But very great care must always be exercised so that no man in a false confidence imagines that by such works he will be justified or acquire merit or be saved; for this is the work of faith alone, as I have repeatedly said.

* * *

Our faith in Christ does not free us from works but from false opinions concerning works, that is, from the foolish presumption that justification is acquired by works. Faith redeems, corrects, and preserves our consciences so that we know that righteousness does not consist in works, although works neither can nor ought to be wanting; just as we cannot be without food and drink and all the works of this mortal body, yet our righteousness is not in them, but in faith; and yet those works of the body are not to be despised or neglected on that account. In this world we are bound by the needs of our bodily life, but we are not righteous because of them. "My kingship is not of this world" [John 18:36], says Christ. He does not, however, say, "My kingship is not here, that is, in this world." And Paul says, "Though we live in the world we are not carrying on a worldly war" [II Cor. 10:3], and in Gal. 2 [:20], "The life I now live in the flesh I live by faith in the Son of God." Thus what we do, live, and are in works and ceremonies, we do because of the necessities of this life and of the effort to rule our body. Nevertheless we are righteous, not in these, but in the faith of the Son of God.

TO THE CHRISTIAN NOBILITY
OF THE GERMAN NATION
CONCERNING THE REFORM
OF THE CHRISTIAN ESTATE

1520

Translated by Charles M. Jacobs

Revised by James Atkinson

In response to colleagues and friends, Luther published this small
book in early August, 1520. It contains a general attack on the
theology of the Roman Catholic Church and an indictment of ecclesiastical abuses. Luther at this time is concerned with reforming
the church, and he suggests that a general council to accomplish
the task should be called by the nobility since the church itself is
unable to do it. Humanists and reformers needed a spokesman in
these matters and Luther filled the need with this widely read and
popular treatise. The text below is from *LW* 44, 123–217 passim.

To His Most Illustrious, Most Mighty, and Imperial Majesty, and to
the Christian Nobility of the German Nation, from Doctor Martin
Luther.

Grace and power from God, Most Illustrious Majesty, and most
gracious and dear lords.

It is not from sheer impertinence or rashness that I, one poor
man, have taken it upon myself to address your worships. All the
estates of Christendom, particularly in Germany, are now oppressed
by distress and affliction, and this has stirred not only me but everybody else to cry out time and time again and to pray for help. It
has even compelled me now at this time to cry aloud that God
may inspire someone with his Spirit to lend a helping hand to this

distressed and wretched nation. Often the councils have made some pretense at reformation,* but their attempts have been cleverly frustrated by the guile of certain men, and things have gone from bad to worse. With God's help I intend to expose the wiles and wickedness of these men, so that they are shown up for what they are and may never again be so obstructive and destructive. God has given us a young man of noble birth as head of state,* and in him has awakened great hopes of good in many hearts. Presented with such an opportunity we ought to apply ourselves and use this time of grace profitably.

The first and most important thing to do in this matter is to prepare ourselves in all seriousness. We must not start something by trusting in great power or human reason, even if all the power in the world were ours. For God cannot and will not suffer that a good work begin by relying upon one's own power and reason. He dashes such works to the ground, they do no good at all. As it says in Psalm 33 [:16], "No king is saved by his great might and no lord is saved by the greatness of his strength." I fear that this is why the good emperors Frederick I and Frederick II and many other German emperors were in former times shamefully oppressed and trodden underfoot by the popes, although all the world feared the emperors. It may be that they relied on their own might more than on God, and therefore had to fall. What was it in our own times that raised the bloodthirsty Julius II* to such heights? Nothing else, I fear, except that France, the Germans, and Venice relied upon themselves. The children of Benjamin slew forty-two thousand Israelites because the latter relied on their own strength, Judges 30 [:21].

That it may not so fare with us and our noble Charles, we must realize that in this matter we are not dealing with men, but with the princes of hell. These princes could fill the world with war and bloodshed, but war and bloodshed do not overcome them. We must tackle this job by renouncing trust in physical force and trusting humbly in God. We must seek God's help through earnest prayer and fix our minds on nothing else than the misery and distress of suffering Christendom without regard to what evil men deserve. Otherwise, we may start the game with great prospects of success, but when we get into it the evil spirits will stir up such confusion that the whole world will swim in blood, and then nothing will come of it all. Let us act wisely, therefore, and in the fear of God. The more force we use, the greater our disaster if we do not act humbly and in the fear of God. If the popes and Romanists have hitherto been able to set kings against each other by the devil's help, they may well be able to do it again if we were to go ahead without the help of God on our own strength and by our own cunning.

The Romanists have very cleverly built three walls around themselves. Hitherto they have protected themselves by these walls in such a way that no one has been able to reform them. As a result, the whole of Christendom has fallen abominably.

In the first place, when pressed by the temporal power they have made decrees and declared that the temporal power had no jurisdiction over them, but that, on the contrary, the spiritual power is above the temporal. In the second place, when the attempt is made to reprove them with the Scriptures, they raise the objection that only the pope may interpret the Scriptures. In the third place, if threatened with a council, their story is that no one may summon a council but the pope.

In this way they have cunningly stolen our three rods from us, that they may go unpunished. They have ensconced themselves within the safe stronghold of these three walls so that they can practice all the knavery and wickedness which we see today. Even when they have been compelled to hold a council they have weakened its power in advance by putting the princes under oath to let them remain as they were. In addition, they have given the pope full authority over all decisions of a council, so that it is all the same whether there are many councils or no councils. They only deceive us with puppet shows and sham fights. They fear terribly for their skin in a really free council! They have so intimidated kings and princes with this technique that they believe it would be an offense against God not to be obedient to the Romanists in all their knavish and ghoulish deceits.

May God help us, and give us just one of those trumpets with which the walls of Jericho were overthrown to blast down these walls of straw and paper in the same way and set free the Christian rods for the punishment of sin, [and] bring to light the craft and deceit of the devil, to the end that through punishment we may reform ourselves and once more attain God's favor.

Let us begin by attacking the first wall. It is pure invention that pope, bishop, priests, and monks are called the spiritual estate while princes, lords, artisans, and farmers are called the temporal estate. This is indeed a piece of deceit and hypocrisy. Yet no one need be intimidated by it, and for this reason: all Christians are truly of the spiritual estate, and there is no difference among them except that of office. Paul says in I Corinthians 12 [:12-13] that we are all one body, yet every member has its own work by which it serves the others. This is because we all have one baptism, one gospel, one faith, and are all Christians alike; for baptism, gospel, and faith alone make us spiritual and a Christian people.

The pope or bishop anoints, shaves heads, ordains, consecrates, and prescribes garb different from that of the laity, but he can never make a man into a Christian or into a spiritual man by so doing. He might well make a man into a hypocrite or a humbug and blockhead, but never a Christian or a spiritual man. As far as that goes, we are all consecrated priests through baptism, as St. Peter says in I Peter 2 [:9], "You are a royal priesthood and a priestly realm." The Apocalypse says, "Thou hast made us to be priests and kings by thy blood" [Rev. 5:9-10]. The consecration by pope or bishop would never make a priest, and if we had no higher consecration than that which pope or bishop gives, no one could say mass or preach a sermon or give absolution.

Therefore, when a bishop consecrates it is nothing else than that in the place and stead of the whole community, all of whom have like power, he takes a person and charges him to exercise this power on behalf of the others. It is like ten brothers, all king's sons and equal heirs, choosing one of themselves to rule the inheritance in the interests of all. In one sense they are all kings and of equal power, and yet one of them is charged with the responsibility of ruling. To put it still more clearly: suppose a group of earnest Christian laymen were taken prisoner and set down in a desert without an episcopally ordained priest among them. And suppose they were to come to a common mind there and then in the desert and elect one of their number, whether he were married or not, and charge him to baptize, say mass, pronounce absolution, and preach the gospel. Such a man would be as truly a priest as though he had been ordained by all the bishops and popes in the world. That is why in cases of necessity anyone can baptize and give absolution. This would be impossible if we were not all priests. Through canon law the Romanists have almost destroyed and made unknown the wondrous grace and authority of baptism and justification. In times gone by Christians used to choose their bishops and priests in this way from among their own number, and they were confirmed in their office by the other bishops without all the fuss that goes on nowadays. St. Augustine, Ambrose, and Cyprian each became [a bishop in this way].

Since those who exercise secular authority have been baptized with the same baptism, and have the same faith and the same gospel as the rest of us, we must admit that they are priests and bishops and we must regard their office as one which has a proper and useful place in the Christian community. For whoever comes out of the water of baptism can boast that he is already a consecrated priest, bishop, and pope, although of course it is not seemly that just anybody should exercise such office. Because we are all priests of equal standing, no one must push himself forward and take it upon himself, without our consent and election, to do that for which we all have equal authority. For no one dare take upon himself what is common to all without the authority and consent of the community. And should it happen that a person chosen for such office were deposed for abuse of trust, he would then be exactly what he was before. Therefore, a priest in Christendom is nothing else but an officeholder. As long as he holds office he takes precedence; where he is deposed, he is a peasant or a townsman like anybody else. Indeed, a priest is never a priest when he is deposed. But now the Romanists have invented *characteres indelebiles** and say that a deposed priest is nevertheless something different from a mere layman. They hold the illusion that a priest can never be anything other than a priest, or ever become a layman. All this is just contrived talk, and human regulation.

It follows from this argument that there is no true, basic difference between laymen and priests, princes and bishops, between religious and secular, except for the sake of office and work, but not for the sake of status. They are all of the spiritual estate, all are truly priests, bishops, and popes. But they do not all have the same work to do. Just as all priests and monks do not have the same work. This is the teaching of St. Paul in Romans 12 [:4-5] and I Corinthians 12 [:12] and in I Peter 2 [:9], as I have said above, namely, that we are all one body of Christ the Head, and all members one of another. Christ does not have two different bodies, one temporal, the other spiritual. There is but one Head and one body.

Therefore, just as those who are now called "spiritual," that is, priests, bishops, or popes, are neither different from other Christians nor superior to them, except that they are charged with the administration of the word of God and the sacraments, which is their work and office, so it is with the temporal authorities. They bear the sword and rod in their hand to punish the wicked and protect the good. A cobbler, a smith, a peasant—each has the work and office of his trade, and yet they are all alike consecrated priests and bishops. Further, everyone must benefit and serve every other by means of his own work or office so that in this way many kinds of work may be done for the bodily and spiritual welfare of the community, just as all the members of the body serve one another [I Cor. 12:14-26].

Consider for a moment how Christian is the decree which says that the temporal power is not above the "spiritual estate" and has no right to punish it. That is as much as to say that the hand shall not help the eye when it suffers pain. Is it not unnatural, not to mention un-Christian, that one member does not help another and prevent its destruction? In fact, the more honorable the member, the more the others ought to help. I say therefore that since the temporal power is ordained of God to punish the wicked and protect the good, it should be left free to perform its office in the whole body of Christendom without restriction and without respect to persons, whether it affects pope, bishops, priests, monks, nuns, or anyone else. If it were right to say that the temporal power is inferior to all the spiritual estates (preacher, confessor, or any spiritual office), and so prevent the temporal power from doing its proper work, then the tailors, cobblers, stonemasons, carpenters, cooks, innkeepers, farmers, and all the temporal craftsmen should be prevented from providing pope, bishops, priests, and monks with shoes, clothes, house, meat and drink, as well as from paying them any tribute. But if these laymen are allowed to do their proper work without restriction, what then are the Romanist scribes doing with their own laws, which exempt them from the jurisdiction of the temporal Christian authority? It is just so that they can be free to do evil and fulfil what St. Peter said, "False teachers will rise up among you who will deceive you, and with their false and fanciful talk, they will take advantage of you" [II Pet. 2:1–3].

For these reasons the temporal Christian authority ought to exercise its office without hindrance, regardless of whether it is pope, bishop, or priest whom it affects. Whoever is guilty, let him suffer. All that canon law has said to the contrary is the invention of Romanist presumption. For thus St. Paul says to all Christians, "Let every soul (I take that to mean the pope's soul also) be subject to the temporal authority; for it does not bear the sword in vain, but serves God by punishing the wicked and benefiting the good" [Rom. 13:1, 4]. St. Peter, too, says, "Be subject to all human ordinances for the sake of the Lord, who so wills it" [I Pet. 2:13, 15]. He has also prophesied in II Peter 2 [:1] that such men would arise and despise the temporal authority. This is exactly what has happened through the canon law.

So, then, I think this first paper wall is overthrown. Inasmuch as the temporal power has become a member of the Christian body it is a spiritual estate, even though its work is physical. Therefore, its work should extend without hindrance to all the members of the whole body to punish and use force whenever guilt deserves or necessity demands, without regard to whether the culprit is pope, bishop, or priest. Let the Romanists hurl threats and bans about as they like. That is why guilty priests, when they are handed over to secular law, are first deprived of their priestly dignities. This would not be right unless the secular sword previously had had authority over these priests by divine right. Moreover, it is intolerable that in canon law so much importance is attached to the freedom, life, and property of the clergy, as though the laity were not also as spiritual and as good Christians as they, or did not also belong to the church. Why are your life and limb, your property and honor, so cheap and mine not, inasmuch as we are all Christians and have the same baptism, the same faith, the same Spirit, and all the rest? If a priest is murdered, the whole country is placed under interdict.* Why not when a peasant is murdered? How does this great difference come about between two men who are both Christians? It comes from the laws and fabrications of men.

Moreover, it can be no good spirit which has invented such exceptions and granted sin such license and impunity. For if it is our duty to strive against the words and works of the devil and to drive him out in whatever way we can, as both Christ and his apostles command us, how have we gotten into such a state that we have to do nothing and say nothing when the pope or his cohorts undertake devilish words and works? Ought we merely out of regard for these people allow the suppression of divine commandments and truth, which we have sworn in baptism to support with life and limb? Then we should have to answer for all the souls that would thereby be abandoned and led astray!

It must, therefore, have been the chief devil himself who said what is written in the canon law, that if the pope were so scandalously bad as to lead crowds of souls to the devil, still he could not be deposed. At Rome they build on this accursed and devilish foundation, and think that we should let all the world go to the devil rather than resist their knavery. If the fact that one man is set over others were sufficient reason why he should not be punished, then no Christian could punish another, since Christ commanded that every man should esteem himself as the lowliest and the least [Matt. 18:4].

Where sin is, there is no longer any shielding from punishment. St. Gregory writes that we are indeed all equal, but guilt makes a man inferior to others. Now we see how the Romanists treat Christendom. They take away its freedom without any proof from Scripture, at their own whim. But God, as well as the apostles, made them subject to the temporal sword. It is to be feared that this is a game of the Antichrist, or at any rate that his forerunner has appeared.

The second wall is still more loosely built and less substantial. The Romanists want to be the only masters of Holy Scripture, although they never learn a thing from the Bible all their life long. They assume the sole authority for themselves, and, quite unashamed, they play about with words before our very eyes, trying to persuade us that the pope cannot err in matters of faith, regardless of whether he is righteous or wicked. Yet they cannot point to a single letter. This is why so many heretical and un-Christian, even unnatural, ordinances stand in the canon law. But there is no need to talk about these ordinances at present. Since these Romanists think the Holy Spirit never leaves them, no matter how ignorant and wicked they are, they become bold and decree only what they want. And if what they claim were true, why have Holy Scripture at all? Of what use is Scripture? Let us burn the Scripture and be satisfied with the unlearned gentlemen at Rome who possess the Holy Spirit! And yet the Holy Spirit can be possessed only by pious hearts. If I had not read the words with my own eyes, I would not have believed it possible for the devil to have made such stupid claims at Rome, and to have won supporters for them.

But so as not to fight them with mere words, we will quote the Scriptures. St. Paul says in I Corinthians 14 [:30], "If something better is revealed to anyone, though he is already sitting and listening to another in God's word, then the one who is speaking shall hold his peace and give place." What would be the point of this commandment if we were compelled to believe only the man who does the talking, or the man who is at the top? Even Christ said in John 6 [:45] that all Christians shall be taught by God. If it were to happen that the pope and his cohorts were wicked and not true Christians, were not taught by God and were without understanding, and at the same time some obscure person had a right understanding, why should the people not follow the obscure man? Has the pope not erred many times? Who would help Christendom when the pope erred if we did not have somebody we could trust more than him, somebody who had the Scriptures on his side?

Therefore, their claim that only the pope may interpret Scripture is an outrageous fancied fable. They cannot produce a single letter [of Scripture] to maintain that the interpretation of Scripture or the confirmation of its interpretation belongs to the pope alone. They themselves have usurped this power. And although they allege that this power was given to St. Peter when the keys were given him, it is clear enough that the keys were not given to Peter alone but to the whole community. Further, the keys were not ordained for doctrine or government, but only for the binding or loosing of sin. Whatever else or whatever more they arrogate to themselves on the basis of the keys is a mere fabrication. But Christ's words to Peter, "I have prayed for you that your faith fail not" [Luke 22:32], cannot be applied to the pope, since the majority of the popes have been without faith, as they must themselves confess. Besides, it is not only for Peter that Christ prayed, but also for all apostles and Christians, as he says in John 17 [:9, 20], "Father, I pray for those whom thou hast given me, and not for these only, but for all who believe on me through their word." Is that not clear enough?

Just think of it! The Romanists must admit that there are among us good Christians who have the true faith, spirit, understanding, word, and mind of Christ. Why, then, should we reject

45

the word and understanding of good Christians and follow the pope, who has neither faith nor the Spirit? To follow the pope would be to deny the whole faith as well as the Christian church. Again, if the article, "I believe in one holy Christian church," is correct, then the pope cannot be the only one who is right. Otherwise, we would have to confess, "I believe in the pope at Rome." This would reduce the Christian church to one man, and be nothing else than a devilish and hellish error.

Besides, if we are all priests, as was said above, and all have one faith, one gospel, one sacrament, why should we not also have the power to test and judge what is right or wrong in matters of faith? What becomes of Paul's words in I Corinthians 2 [:15], "A spiritual man judges all things, yet he is judged by no one"? And II Corinthians 4 [:13], "We all have one spirit of faith"? Why, then, should not we perceive what is consistent with faith and what is not, just as well as an unbelieving pope does?

We ought to become bold and free on the authority of all these texts, and many others. We ought not to allow the Spirit of freedom (as Paul calls him [II Cor. 3:17]) to be frightened off by the fabrications of the popes, but we ought to march boldly forward and test all that they do, or leave undone, by our believing understanding of the Scriptures. We must compel the Romanists to follow not their own interpretation but the better one. Long ago Abraham had to listen to Sarah, although she was in more complete subjection to him than we are to anyone on earth [Gen. 21:12]. And Balaam's ass was wiser than the prophet himself [Num. 22:21-35]. If God spoke then through an ass against a prophet, why should he not be able even now to speak through a righteous man against the pope? Similarly, St. Paul rebukes St. Peter as a man in error in Galatians 2 [:11-12]. Therefore, it is the duty of every Christian to espouse the cause of the faith, to understand and defend it, and to denounce every error.

The third wall falls of itself when the first two are down. When the pope acts contrary to the Scriptures, it is our duty to stand by the Scriptures, to reprove him and to constrain him, according to the word of Christ, Matthew 18 [:15-17], "If your brother sins against you, go and tell it to him, between you and him alone; if he does not listen to you, then take one or two others with you; if he does not listen to them, tell it to the church; if he does not listen to the church, consider him a heathen." Here every member is commanded to care for every other. How much more should we do this when the member that does evil is responsible for the government of the church, and by his evil-doing is the cause of much harm and offense to the rest! But if I am to accuse him before the church, I must naturally call the church together.

The Romanists have no basis in Scripture for their claim that the pope alone has the right to call or confirm a council. This is just their own ruling, and it is only valid as long as it is not harmful to Christendom or contrary to the laws of God. Now when the pope deserves punishment, this ruling no longer obtains, for not to punish him by authority of a council is harmful to Christendom.

Thus we read in Acts 15 that it was not St. Peter who called the Apostolic Council but the apostles and elders. If then that right had belonged to St. Peter alone, the council would not have been a Christian council, but a heretical *conciliabulum*.* Even the Council of Nicaea, the most famous of all councils, was neither called nor confirmed by the bishop of Rome, but by the emperor Constantine. Many other emperors after him have done the same, and yet these councils were the most Christian of all. But if the pope alone has the right to convene councils, then these councils would all have been heretical. Further, when I examine the councils the pope did summon, I find that they did nothing of special importance.

Therefore, when necessity demands it, and the pope is an offense to Christendom, the first man who is able should, as a true member of the whole body, do what he can to bring about a truly free council. No one can do this so well as the temporal authorities, especially since they are also fellow-Christians, fellow-priests, fellow-members of the spiritual estate, fellow-lords over all things. Whenever it is necessary or profitable they ought to exercise the office and work which they have received from God over everyone. Would it not be unnatural if a fire broke out in a city and everybody were to stand by and let it burn on and on and consume everything that could burn because nobody had the authority of the mayor, or because, perhaps, the fire broke out in the mayor's house? In such a situation is it not the duty of every citizen to arouse and summon the rest? How much more should this be done in the spiritual city of Christ if a fire of offense breaks out, whether in the papal government, or anywhere else! The same argument holds if an enemy were to attack a city. The man who first roused the others deserves honor and gratitude. Why, then, should he not deserve honor who makes known the presence of the enemy from hell and rouses Christian people and calls them together?

But all their boasting about an authority which dare not be opposed amounts to nothing at all. Nobody in Christendom has authority to do injury or to forbid the resisting of injury. There is no authority in the church except to promote good. Therefore, if the pope were to use his authority to prevent the calling of a free council, thereby preventing the improvement of the church, we should have regard neither for him nor for his authority. And if he were to hurl his bans and thunderbolts, we should despise his conduct as that of a madman. On the contrary, we should excommunicate him and drive him out as best we could, relying completely upon God. This presumptuous authority of his is nothing. He does not even have such authority. He is quickly defeated by a single text of Scripture, where Paul says to the Corinthians, "God has given us authority not to ruin Christendom, but to build it up" [II Cor. 10:8]. Who wants to leap over the hurdle of this text? It is the power of the devil and of Antichrist which resists the things that serve to build up Christendom. Such power is not to be obeyed, but rather resisted with life, property, and with all our might and main.

Even though a miracle were to be done against the temporal authority on the pope's behalf, or if somebody were struck down by the plague—which they boast has sometimes happened—it should be considered as nothing but the work of the devil designed to destroy our faith in God. Christ foretold this in Matthew 24 [:24], "False Christs and false prophets shall come in my name, who shall perform signs and wonders in order to deceive even the elect." And Paul says in II Thessalonians 2 [:9] that Antichrist shall, through the power of Satan, be mighty in false wonders.

Let us, therefore, hold fast to this: no Christian authority can do anything against Christ. As St. Paul says, "We can do nothing against Christ, only for Christ" [II Cor. 13:8]. But if an authority does anything against Christ, then that authority is the power of Antichrist and of the devil, even if it were to deluge us with wonders and plagues. Wonders and plagues prove nothing, especially in these evil latter days. The whole of Scripture foretells such false wonders. This is why we must hold fast to the word of God with firm faith, and then the devil will soon drop his miracles!

With this I hope that all this wicked and lying terror with which the Romanists have long intimidated and dulled our conscience has been overcome, and that they, just like all of us, shall be made subject to the sword. They have no right to interpret Scripture merely by authority and without learning. They have no authority to prevent a council, or even worse yet at their mere whim to pledge it, impose conditions on it, or deprive it of its freedom. When they do that they are truly in the fellowship of Antichrist and the devil. They have nothing at all of Christ except the name.

TEMPORAL AUTHORITY:
TO WHAT EXTENT
IT SHOULD BE OBEYED

1523

Translated by J. J. Schindel

Revised by Walther I. Brandt

At Worms in 1521 Luther was commanded by the highest temporal
authority, the emperor, to recant his works, and he had refused.
Several rulers had burned his works and imprisoned his followers,
and Luther himself had been excommunicated and was under the
ban of the empire. In the midst of these political consequences of
the Reformation, Luther gave some sermons on temporal authority
in October, 1522, before Duke John of Saxony and others who
urged him to publish his thoughts on the subject. Luther then wrote
this relatively nonpolemical treatise in order to provide for the
Christian a general theory of temporal authority. In it Luther explains the nature of temporal authority, its limitations, and the
responsibilities of the Christian subject and the Christian ruler. The
text below is from *LW* 45, 81–129 passim.

First, we must provide a sound basis for the civil law and
sword so no one will doubt that it is in the world by God's will
and ordinance. The passages which do this are the following:
Romans 13, "Let every soul [*seele*] be subject to the governing
authority, for there is no authority except from God; the authority
which everywhere [*allenthalben*] exists has been ordained by God.
He then who resists the governing authority resists the ordinance
of God, and he who resists God's ordinance will incur judgment."
Again, in I Peter 2 [:13-14], "Be subject to every kind of human
ordinance, whether it be to the king as supreme, or to governors,

as those who have been sent by him to punish the wicked and to praise the righteous."

The law of this temporal sword has existed from the beginning of the world. For when Cain slew his brother Abel, he was in such great terror of being killed in turn that God even placed a special prohibition on it and suspended the sword for his sake, so that no one was to slay him [Gen. 4:14-15]. He would not have had this fear if he had not seen and heard from Adam that murderers are to be slain. Moreover, after the Flood, God reestablished and confirmed this in unmistakable terms when he said in Genesis 9 [:6], "Whoever sheds the blood of man, by man shall his blood be shed." This cannot be understood as a plague or punishment of God upon murderers, for many murderers who are punished in other ways or pardoned altogether   continue to live, and eventually die by means other than the sword. Rather, it is said of the law of the sword, that a murderer is guilty of death and in justice is to be slain by the sword. Now if justice should be hindered or the sword have become negligent so that the murderer dies a natural death, Scripture is not on that account false when it says, "Whoever sheds the blood of man, by man shall his blood be shed." The credit or blame belongs to men if this law instituted by God is not carried out; just as other commandments of God, too, are broken.

Afterward it was also confirmed by the law of Moses, Exodus 21 [:14], "If a man wilfully kills another, you shall take him from my altar, that he may die." And again, in the same chapter, "A life for a life, an eye for an eye, a tooth for a tooth, a foot for a foot, a hand for a hand, a wound for a wound, a stripe for a stripe." In addition, Christ also confirms it when he says to Peter in the garden, "He that takes the sword will perish by the sword" [Matt. 26:52], which is to be interpreted exactly like the Genesis 9 [:6] passage, "Whoever sheds the blood of man," etc. Christ is undoubtedly referring in these words to that very passage which he thereby wishes to cite and to confirm. John the Baptist also teaches the same thing. When the soldiers asked him what they should do, he answered, "Do neither violence nor injustice to any one, and be content with your wages" [Luke 3:14]. If the sword were not a godly estate, he should have directed them to get out of it, since he was supposed to make the people perfect and instruct them in a proper Christian way.   Hence, it is certain and clear enough that it is God's will that the temporal sword and law be used for the punishment of the wicked and the protection of the upright.

Second. There appear to be powerful arguments to the contrary. Christ says in Matthew 5 [:38-41], "You have heard that it was said to them of old: An eye for an eye, a tooth for a tooth. But I say to you, Do not resist evil; but if anyone strikes you on the right cheek, turn to him the other also. And if anyone would sue you and take your coat, let him have your cloak as well. And if anyone forces you to go one mile, go with him two miles," etc. Likewise Paul in Romans 12 [:19], "Beloved, defend not yourselves, but leave it to the wrath of God; for it is written, 'Vengeance is mine; I will repay, says the Lord.'" And in Matthew 5 [:44], "Love your enemies, do good to them that hate you." And again, in I Peter 2 [3:9], "Do not return evil for evil, or reviling for reviling," etc. These and similar passages would certainly make it appear as though in the New Testament Christians were to have no temporal sword.

Hence, the sophists also say that Christ has thereby abolished the law of Moses. Of such commandments they make "counsels" for the perfect. They divide Christian teaching and Christians into two classes. One part they call the perfect, and assign to it such counsels. The other they call the imperfect, and assign to it the commandments. This they do out of sheer wantonness and caprice, without any scriptural basis. They fail to see that in the same passage Christ lays such stress on his teaching that he is unwilling to have the least word of it set aside, and condemns to hell those who do not love their enemies. Therefore, we must interpret these passages differently, so that Christ's words may apply to everyone alike, be he perfect or imperfect. For perfection and imperfection do not consist in works, and do not establish any distinct external order among Christians. They exist in the heart, in faith and love, so that those who believe and love the most are the perfect ones, whether they be outwardly male or female, prince or peasant, monk or layman. For love and faith produce no sects or outward differences.

Third. Here we must divide the children of Adam and all mankind into two classes, the first belonging to the kingdom of God, the second to the kingdom of the world. Those who belong to the kingdom of God are all the true believers who are in Christ and under Christ, for Christ is King and Lord in the kingdom of God, as Psalm 2 [:6] and all of Scripture says. For this reason he came into the world, that he might begin God's kingdom and establish it in the world. Therefore, he says before Pilate, "My kingdom is not of the world, but every one who is of the truth hears my voice" [John 18:36-37]. In the gospel he continually refers to the kingdom of God, and says, "Amend your ways, the kingdom of God is at hand" [Matt. 4:17, 10:7]; again, "Seek first the kingdom of God and his righteousness" [Matt. 6:33]. He also calls the gospel a gospel of the kingdom of God; because it teaches, governs, and upholds God's kingdom.

Now observe, these people need no temporal law or sword. If all the world were composed of real Christians, that is, true believers, there would be no need for or benefits from prince, king, lord, sword, or law. They would serve no purpose, since Christians have in their heart the Holy Spirit, who both teaches and makes them to do injustice to no one, to love everyone, and to suffer injustice and even death willingly and cheerfully at the hands of anyone. Where there is nothing but the unadulterated doing of right and bearing of wrong, there is no need for any suit, litigation, court, judge, penalty, law, or sword. For this reason it is impossible that the temporal sword and law should find any work to do among Christians, since they do of their own accord much more than all laws and teachings can demand, just as Paul says in I Timothy 1 [:9], "The law is not laid down for the just but for the lawless."

Why is this? It is because the righteous man of his own accord does all and more than the law demands. But the unrighteous do nothing that the law demands; therefore, they need the law to instruct, constrain, and compel them to do good. A good tree needs no instruction or law to bear good fruit; its nature causes it to bear according to its kind without any law or instruction. I would take to be quite a fool any man who would make a book full of laws and statutes for an apple tree telling it how to bear apples and not thorns, when the tree is able by its own nature to do this better than the man with all his books can describe and demand. Just so, by the Spirit and by faith all Christians are so thoroughly disposed and conditioned in their very nature that they do right and keep the law better than one can teach them with all manner of statutes; so far as they themselves are concerned, no statutes or laws are needed.

You ask: Why, then, did God give so many commandments to all mankind, and why does Christ prescribe in the gospel so many things for us to do? Of this I have written at length in the Postils * and elsewhere. To put it here as briefly as possible, Paul says that the law has been laid down for the sake of the lawless [I Tim. 1:9], that is, so that those who are not Christians may through the law be restrained outwardly from evil deeds, as we shall hear later. Now since no one is by nature Christian or righteous, but altogether sinful and wicked, God through the law puts them all under restraint so they dare not wilfully implement their wickedness in actual deeds. In addition, Paul ascribes to the law another function in Romans 7 and Galatians 2, that of teaching men to recognize sin in order that it may make them humble unto grace and unto faith in Christ. Christ does the same thing here in Matthew 5 [:39], where he teaches that we should not resist evil; by this he is interpreting the law and teaching what ought to be and must be the state and temper of a true Christian, as we shall hear further later on.

Fourth. All who are not Christians belong to the kingdom of the world and are under the law. There are few true believers, and still fewer who live a Christian life, who do not resist evil and indeed themselves do no evil. For this reason God has provided for them a different government beyond the Christian estate and kingdom of God. He has subjected them to the sword so that, even though they would like to, they are unable to practice their wickedness, and if they do practice it they cannot do so without fear or with success and impunity. In the same way a savage wild beast is bound with chains and ropes so that it cannot bite and tear as it would normally do, even though it would like to; whereas a tame and gentle animal needs no restraint, but is harmless despite the lack of chains and ropes.

If this were not so, men would devour one another, seeing that the whole world is evil and that among thousands there is scarcely a single true Christian. No one could support wife and child, feed himself, and serve God. The world would be reduced to chaos. For this reason God has ordained two governments: the spiritual, by which the Holy Spirit produces Christians and righteous people under Christ; and the temporal, which restrains the

un-Christian and wicked so that—no thanks to them—they are
obliged to keep still and to maintain an outward peace. Thus
does St. Paul interpret the temporal sword in Romans 13 [:3],
when he says it is not a terror to good conduct but to bad. And
Peter says it is for the punishment of the wicked [I Pet. 2:14].

If anyone attempted to rule the world by the gospel and
to abolish all temporal law and sword on the plea that all are
baptized and Christian, and that, according to the gospel, there
shall be among them no law or sword—or need for either—pray
tell me, friend, what would he be doing? He would be loosing
the ropes and chains of the savage wild beasts and letting them
bite and mangle everyone, meanwhile insisting that they were
harmless, tame, and gentle creatures; but I would have the proof
in my wounds. Just so would the wicked under the name of
Christian abuse evangelical freedom, carry on their rascality, and
insist that they were Christians subject neither to law nor sword,
as some are already raving and ranting.

To such a one we must say: Certainly it is true that Christians, so far as they themselves are concerned, are subject neither
to law nor sword, and have need of neither. But take heed and
first fill the world with real Christians before you attempt to rule it
in a Christian and evangelical manner. This you will never accomplish; for the world and the masses are and always will be
un-Christian, even if they are all baptized and Christian in name.
Christians are few and far between (as the saying is). Therefore,
it is out of the question that there should be a common Christian
government over the whole world, or indeed over a single country
or any considerable body of people, for the wicked always out-
number the good. Hence, a man who would venture to govern
an entire country or the world with the gospel would be like a
shepherd who should put together in one fold wolves, lions,
eagles, and sheep, and let them mingle freely with one another,
saying, "Help yourselves, and be good and peaceful toward one
another. The fold is open, there is plenty of food. You need have
no fear of dogs and clubs." The sheep would doubtless keep the
peace and allow themselves to be fed and governed peacefully,
but they would not live long, nor would one beast survive another.

For this reason one must carefully distinguish between these
two governments. Both must be permitted to remain; the one to
produce righteousness, the other to bring about external peace

and prevent evil deeds. Neither one is sufficient in the world without the other.

* * *

Fifth. But you say: if Christians then do not need the temporal sword or law, why does Paul say to all Christians in Romans 13 [:1], "Let all souls be subject to the governing authority," and St. Peter, "Be subject to every human ordinance" [I Pet. 2:13], etc., as quoted above? Answer: I have just said that Christians, among themselves and by and for themselves, need no law or sword, since it is neither necessary nor useful for them. Since a true Christian lives and labors on earth not for himself alone but for his neighbor, he does by the very nature of his spirit even what he himself has no need of, but is needful and useful to his neighbor. Because the sword is most beneficial and necessary for the whole world in order to preserve peace, punish sin, and restrain the wicked, the Christian submits most willingly to the rule of the sword, pays his taxes, honors those in authority, serves, helps, and does all he can to assist the governing authority, that it may continue to function and be held in honor and fear. Although he has no need of these things for himself—to him they are not essential—nevertheless, he concerns himself about what is serviceable and of benefit to others, as Paul teaches in Ephesians 5 [:21–6:9].

Just as he performs all other works of love which he himself does not need—he does not visit the sick in order that he himself may be made well, or feed others because he himself needs food—so he serves the governing authority not because he needs it but for the sake of others, that they may be protected and that the wicked may not become worse.

* * *

Sixth. You ask whether a Christian too may bear the temporal sword and punish the wicked, since Christ's words, "Do not resist evil," are so clear and definite that the sophists have had to make of them a "counsel." Answer: You have now heard two propositions. One is that the sword can have no place among Christians; therefore, you cannot bear it among Christians or hold it over them, for they do not need it. The question, therefore, must be referred to the other group, the non-Christians, whether you may bear it there in a Christian manner. Here the other proposition applies, that you are under obligation to serve and assist the sword by whatever means you can, with body, goods, honor, and soul. For it is something which you do not need, but which is very beneficial and essential for the whole world and for your neighbor. Therefore, if you see that there is a lack of hangmen, constables, judges, lords, or princes, and you find that you are qualified, you should offer your services and seek the position, that the essential governmental authority may not be despised and become enfeebled or perish. The world cannot and dare not dispense with it.

* * *

To prove our position also by the New Testament, the testimony of John the Baptist in Luke 3 [:14] stands unshaken on this point. There can be no doubt that it was his task to point to Christ, witness for him, and teach about him; that is to say, the teaching of the man who was to lead a truly perfected people to Christ had of necessity to be purely New Testament and evangelical. John confirms the soldiers' calling, saying they should be content with their wages. Now if it had been un-Christian to bear the sword, he ought to have censured them for it and told them to abandon both wages and sword, else he would not have been teaching them Christianity aright. So likewise, when St. Peter in Acts 10 [:34-43] preached Christ to Cornelius, he did not tell him to abandon his profession, which he would have had to do if it had prevented Cornelius from being a Christian. Moreover, before he was baptized the Holy Spirit came upon him [Acts 10:44-48]. St. Luke also praises him as an upright man prior to St. Peter's sermon, and does not criticize him for being a soldier, the centurion of a pagan emperor [Acts 10:1-2]. It is only right that what the Holy Spirit permitted to remain and did not censure in the case of Cornelius, we too should permit and not censure.

* * *

Here you see that Christ is not abrogating the law when he says, "You have heard that it was said to them of old, 'An eye for an eye'; but I say to you: Do not resist evil," etc. [Matt. 5:38-39]. On the contrary, he is expounding the meaning of the law as it is to be understood, as if he were to say, "You Jews think that it is right and proper in the sight of God to recover by law what is yours. You rely on what Moses said, 'An eye for an eye,' etc. But I say to you that Moses set this law over the wicked, who do not belong to God's kingdom, in order that they might not avenge themselves or do worse but be compelled by such outward law to desist from evil, in order that by outward law and rule they might be kept subordinate to the governing authority. You, however, should so conduct yourselves that you neither need nor resort to such law. Although the temporal authority must have such a law by which to judge unbelievers, and although you yourselves may also use it for judging others, still you should not invoke or use it for yourselves and in your own affairs. You have the kingdom of heaven; therefore, you should leave the kingdom of earth to anyone who wants to take it."

There you see that Christ does not interpret his words to mean that he is abrogating the law of Moses or prohibiting temporal authority. He is rather making an exception of his own people. They are not to use the secular authority for themselves but leave it to unbelievers. Yet they may also serve these unbelievers, even with their own law, since they are not Christians and no one can be forced into Christianity. That Christ's words apply only to his own is evident from the fact that later on he says they should love their enemies and be perfect like their heavenly Father [Matt. 5:44, 48]. But he who loves his enemies and is perfect leaves the law alone and does not use it to demand an eye for an eye. Neither does he restrain the non-Christians, however, who do not love their enemies and who do wish to make use of the law; indeed, he lends his help that these laws may hinder the wicked from doing worse.

Thus the word of Christ is now reconciled, I believe, with the passages which establish the sword, and the meaning is this: No Christian shall wield or invoke the sword for himself and his cause. In behalf of another, however, he may and should wield it and invoke it to restrain wickedness and to defend godliness. Even as the Lord says in the same chapter [Matt. 5:34-37], "A Christian should not swear, but his word should be Yes, yes; No, no." That is, for himself and of his own volition and desire, he should not swear. When it is needful or necessary, however, and salvation or the honor of God demands it, he should swear. Thus, he uses the forbidden oath to serve another, just as he uses the forbidden sword to serve another. Christ and Paul often swore in order to make their teaching and testimony valuable and credible to others, as men do and have the right to do in covenants and compacts, etc., of which Psalm 63 [:11] says, "They shall be praised who swear by his name."

Here you inquire further, whether constables, hangmen, jurists, lawyers, and others of similar function can also be Christians and in a state of salvation. Answer: If the governing authority and its sword are a divine service, as was proved above, then everything that is essential for the authority's bearing of the sword must also be divine service. There must be those who arrest, prosecute, execute, and destroy the wicked, and who protect, acquit, defend, and save the good. Therefore, when they perform their duties, not with the intention of seeking their own ends but only of helping the law and the governing authority function to coerce the wicked, there is no peril in that; they may use their office like anybody else would use his trade, as a means of livelihood. For, as has been said, love of neighbor is not concerned about its own; it considers not how great or humble, but how profitable and needful the works are for neighbor or community.

You may ask, "Why may I not use the sword for myself and for my own cause, so long as it is my intention not to seek my own advantage but to punish evil?" Answer: Such a miracle is not impossible, but very rare and hazardous. Where the Spirit is so richly present it may well happen. For we read thus of Samson in Judges 15 [:11], that he said, "As they did to me, so have I done to them," even though Proverbs 24 [:29] says to the contrary, "Do not say, I will do to him as he has done to me," and Proverbs 20 [:22] adds, "Do not say, I will repay him his evil." Samson was called of God to harass the Philistines and deliver the children of Israel. Although he used them as an occasion to further his own cause, still he did not do so in order to avenge himself or to seek his own interests, but to serve others and to punish the Philistines [Judg. 14:4]. No one but a true Christian, filled with the Spirit, will follow this example. Where reason too tries to do likewise, it will probably contend that it is not trying to seek its own, but this will be basically untrue, for it cannot be done without grace. Therefore first become like Samson, and then you can also do as Samson did.

Part Two
How Far Temporal Authority Extends

We come now to the main part of this treatise. Having learned that there must be temporal authority on earth, and how it is to be exercised in a Christian and salutary manner, we must now learn how far its arm extends and how widely its hand stretches, lest it extend too far and encroach upon God's kingdom and government. It is essential for us to know this, for where it is given too wide a scope, intolerable and terrible injury follows; on the other hand, injury is also inevitable where it is restricted too narrowly. In the former case, the temporal authority punishes too much; in the latter case, it punishes too little. To err in this direction, however, and punish too little is more tolerable, for it is always better to let a scoundrel live than to put a godly man to death. The world has plenty of scoundrels anyway and must continue to have them, but godly men are scarce.

It is to be noted first that the two classes of Adam's children—the one in God's kingdom under Christ and the other in the kingdom of the world under the governing authority, as was said above—have two kinds of law. For every kingdom must have its own laws and statutes; without law no kingdom or government can survive, as everyday experience amply shows. The temporal government has laws which extend no further than to life and property and external affairs on earth, for God cannot and will not permit anyone but himself to rule over the soul. Therefore, where the temporal authority presumes to prescribe laws for the soul, it encroaches upon God's government and only misleads souls and destroys them. We want to make this so clear that everyone will grasp it, and that our fine gentlemen, the princes and bishops, will see what fools they are when they seek to coerce the people with their laws and commandments into believing this or that.

* * *

Furthermore, every man runs his own risk in believing as he does, and he must see to it himself that he believes rightly. As nobody else can go to heaven or hell for me, so nobody else can believe or disbelieve for me; as nobody else can open or close heaven or hell to me, so nobody else can drive me to belief or unbelief. How he believes or disbelieves is a matter for the conscience of each individual, and since this takes nothing away from the temporal authority the latter should be content to attend to its own affairs and let men believe this or that as they are able and willing, and constrain no one by force. For faith is a free act, to which no one can be forced. Indeed, it is a work of God in the spirit, not something which outward authority should compel or create. Hence arises the common saying, found also in Augustine, "No one can or ought to be forced to believe."

Moreover, the blind, wretched fellows fail to see how utterly hopeless and impossible a thing they are attempting. For no matter how harshly they lay down the law, or how violently they rage, they can do no more than force an outward compliance of the mouth and the hand; the heart they cannot compel, though they work themselves to a frazzle. For the proverb is true: "Thoughts are tax-free." Why do they persist in trying to force people to believe from the heart when they see that it is impossible? In so doing they only compel weak consciences to lie, to disavow, and to utter what is not in their hearts. They thereby load themselves down with dreadful alien sins, for all the lies and false confessions which such weak consciences utter fall back upon him who compels them. Even if their subjects were in error, it would be much easier simply to let them err than to compel them to lie and to utter what is not in their hearts. In addition, it is not right to prevent evil by something even worse.

* * *

If your prince or temporal ruler commands you to side with the pope, to believe thus and so, or to get rid of certain books, you should say, "It is not fitting that Lucifer should sit at the side of God. Gracious sir, I owe you obedience in body and property; command me within the limits of your authority on earth, and I will obey. But if you command me to believe or to get rid of certain books, I will not obey; for then you are a tyrant and overreach yourself, commanding where you have neither the right nor the authority," etc. Should he seize your property on account of this and punish such disobedience, then blessed are you; thank God that you are worthy to suffer for the sake of the divine word. Let him rage, fool that he is; he will meet his judge. For I tell you, if you fail to withstand him, if you give in to him and let him take away your faith and your books, you have truly denied God.

* * *

You must know that since the beginning of the world a wise prince is a mighty rare bird, and an upright prince even rarer. They are generally the biggest fools or the worst scoundrels on earth; therefore, one must constantly expect the worst from them and look for little good, especially in divine matters which concern the salvation of souls. They are God's executioners and hangmen; his divine wrath uses them to punish the wicked and to maintain outward peace. Our God is a great lord and ruler; this is why he must also have such noble, highborn, and rich hangmen and constables. He desires that everyone shall copiously accord them riches, honor, and fear in abundance. It pleases his divine will that we call his hangmen gracious lords, fall at their feet, and be subject to them in all humility, so long as they do not ply their trade too far and try to become shepherds instead of hangmen. If a prince should happen to be wise, upright, or a Christian, that is one of the great miracles, the most precious token of divine grace upon that land. Ordinarily the course of events is in accordance with the passage from Isaiah 3 [:4], "I will make boys their princes, and gaping fools shall rule over them"; and in Hosea 13 [:11], "I will give you a king in my anger, and take him away in my wrath." The world is too wicked, and does not deserve to have many wise and upright princes. Frogs must have their storks.*

Again you say, "The temporal power is not forcing men to believe; it is simply seeing to it externally that no one deceives the people by false doctrine; how could heretics otherwise be restrained?" Answer: This the bishops should do; it is a function entrusted to them and not to the princes. Heresy can never be restrained by force. One will have to tackle the problem in some other way, for heresy must be opposed and dealt with otherwise than with the sword. Here God's word must do the fighting. If it does not succeed, certainly the temporal power will not succeed either, even if it were to drench the world in blood. Heresy is a spiritual matter which you cannot hack to pieces with iron, consume with fire, or drown in water. God's word alone avails here, as Paul says in II Corinthians 10 [:4-5], "Our weapons are not carnal, but mighty in God to destroy every argument and proud obstacle that exalts itself against the knowledge of God, and to take every thought captive in the service of Christ."

* * *

But you might say, "Since there is to be no temporal sword among Christians, how then are they to be ruled outwardly? There certainly must be authority even among Christians." Answer: Among Christians there shall and can be no authority; rather all are alike subject to one another, as Paul says in Romans 12: "Each shall consider the other his superior";   and Peter says in I Peter 5 [:5], "All of you be subject to one another." This is also what Christ means in Luke 14 [:10], "When you are invited to a wedding, go and sit in the lowest place." Among Christians there is no superior but Christ himself, and him alone. What kind of authority can there be where all are equal and have the same right, power, possession, and honor, and where no one desires to be the other's superior, but each the other's subordinate? Where there are such people, one could not establish authority even if he wanted to, since in the nature of things it is impossible to have superiors where no one is able or willing to be a superior. Where there are no such people, however, there are no real Christians either.

What, then, are the priests and bishops? Answer: Their government is not a matter of authority or power, but a service and an office, for they are neither higher nor better than other Christians.   Therefore, they should impose no law or decree on others without their will and consent. Their ruling is rather nothing more than the inculcating of God's word, by which they guide Christians and overcome heresy. As we have said, Christians can be ruled by nothing except God's word, for Christians must be ruled in faith, not with outward works. Faith, however, can come through no word of man, but only through the word of God, as Paul says in Romans 10 [:17], "Faith comes through hearing, and hearing through the word of God." Those who do not believe are not Christians; they do not belong to Christ's kingdom, but to the worldly kingdom where they are constrained and governed by the sword and by outward rule. Christians do every good thing of their own accord and without constraint, and find God's word alone sufficient for them. Of this I have written frequently and at length elsewhere.

Part Three

Now that we know the limits of temporal authority, it is time to inquire also how a prince should use it. We do this for the sake of those very few who would also like very much to be Christian princes and lords, and who desire to enter into the life in heaven.

* * *

First. He must give consideration and attention to his subjects, and really devote himself to it. This he does when he directs his every thought to making himself useful and beneficial to them; when instead of thinking, "The land and people belong to me, I will do what best pleases me," he thinks rather, "I belong to the land and the people, I shall do what is good for them . . .

* * *

Second. He must beware of the high and mighty and of his counselors, and so conduct himself toward them that he despises none, but also trusts none enough to leave everything to him. God cannot tolerate either course.

* * *

Third. He must take care to deal justly with evildoers. Here he must be very wise and prudent, so he can inflict punishment without injury to others.   . . . Therefore, he must not follow the advice of those counselors and fire-eaters who would stir and incite him to start a war, saying, "What, must we suffer such insult and injustice?" He is a mighty poor Christian who for the sake of a single castle would put the whole land in jeopardy.

In short, here one must go by the proverb, "He cannot govern who cannot wink at faults."   Let this be his rule: Where wrong cannot be punished without greater wrong, there let him waive his rights, however just they may be. He should not have regard to his own injury, but to the wrong others must suffer in consequence of the penalty he imposes. What have the many women and children done to deserve being made widows and orphans in order that you may avenge yourself on a worthless tongue or an evil hand which has injured you?

Here you will ask: "Is a prince then not to go to war, and are his subjects not to follow him into battle?" Answer: This is a far-reaching question, but let me answer it very briefly. To act here as a Christian, I say, a prince should not go to war against his overlord—king, emperor, or other liege lord —but let him who takes, take. For the governing authority must not be resisted by force, but only by confession of the truth. If it is influenced by this, well and good; if not, you are excused, you suffer wrong for God's sake. If, however, the antagonist is your equal, your inferior, or of a foreign government, you should first offer him justice and peace, as Moses taught the children of Israel. If he refuses, then—mindful of what is best for you   —defend yourself against force by force, as Moses so well describes it in Deuteronomy 20 [:10-12]. But in doing this you must not consider your personal interests and how you may remain lord, but those of your subjects to whom you owe help and protection, that such action may proceed in love. Since your entire land is in peril you must make the venture, so that with God's help all may not be lost. If you cannot prevent some from becoming widows and orphans as a consequence, you must at least see that not everything goes to ruin until there is nothing left except widows and orphans.

In this matter subjects are in duty bound to follow, and to devote their life and property, for in such a case one must risk his goods and himself for the sake of others. In a war of this sort it is both Christian and an act of love to kill the enemy without hesitation, to plunder and burn and injure him by every method of warfare   until he is conquered (except that one must beware of sin, and not violate wives and virgins). And when victory has been achieved, one should offer mercy and peace to those who surrender and humble themselves...

What if a prince is in the wrong? Are his people bound to follow him then too? Answer: No, for it is no one's duty to do wrong; we must obey God (who desires the right) rather than men [Acts 5:29]. What if the subjects do not know whether their prince is in the right or not? Answer: So long as they do not know, and cannot with all possible diligence find out, they may obey him without peril to their souls. For in such a case one must apply the law of Moses in Exodus 21,   where he writes that a murderer who has unknowingly and unintentionally killed a man shall through flight to a city of refuge and by judgment of a court be declared acquitted. Whichever side then suffers defeat, whether it be in the right or in the wrong, must accept it as a punishment from God. Whichever side fights and wins in such ignorance, however, must regard its battle as though someone fell from a roof and killed another, and leave the matter to God. It is all the same to God whether he deprives you of life and property by a just or by an unjust lord. You are His creature and He can do with you as He wills, just so your conscience is clear. Thus in Genesis 20 [:2-7] God himself excuses Abimelech for taking Abraham's wife; not because he had done right, but because he had not known that she was Abraham's wife.

Fourth. Here we come to what should really have been placed first, and of which we spoke above. A prince must act in a Christian way toward his God also; that is, he must subject himself to him in entire confidence and pray for wisdom to rule well, as Solomon did [I Kings 3:9]. But of faith and trust in God I have written so much that it is not necessary to say more here. Therefore, we will close with this brief summation, that a prince's duty is fourfold: First, toward God there must be true confidence and earnest prayer; second, toward his subjects there must be love and Christian service; third, with respect to his counselors and officials he must maintain an untrammeled reason and unfettered judgment; fourth, with respect to evildoers he must manifest a restrained severity and firmness. Then the prince's job will be done right, both outwardly and inwardly; it will be pleasing to God and to the people. But he will have to expect much envy and sorrow on account of it; the cross will soon rest on the shoulders of such a prince.

Finally, I must add an appendix in answer to those who raise questions about restitution, that is, about the return of goods wrongfully acquired. This is a matter about which the temporal sword is commonly concerned; much has been written about it, and many fantastically severe judgments have been sought in cases of this sort. I will put it all in a few words, however, and at one fell swoop dispose of all such laws and of the harsh judgments based upon them, thus: No surer law can be found in this matter than the law of love. In the first place, when a case of this sort is brought before you in which one is to make restitution to another, if they are both Christians the matter is soon settled; neither will withhold what belongs to the other, and neither will demand that it be returned. If only one of them is a Christian, namely, the one to whom restitution is due, it is again easy to settle, for he does not care whether restitution is ever made to him. The same is true if the one who is supposed to make restitution is a Christian, for he will do so.

But whether one be a Christian or not a Christian, you should decide the question of restitution as follows. If the debtor is poor and unable to make restitution, and the other party is not poor, then you should let the law of love prevail and acquit the debtor; for according to the law of love the other party is in any event obliged to relinquish the debt and, if necessary, to give him something besides. But if the debtor is not poor, then have him restore as much as he can, whether it be all, a half, a third, or a fourth of it, provided that you leave him enough to assure a house, food, and clothing for himself, his wife, and his children. This much you would owe him in any case, if you could afford it; so much the less ought you to take it away now, since you do not need it and he cannot get along without it.

* * *

A good and just decision must not and cannot be pronounced out of books, but must come from a free mind, as though there were no books. Such a free decision is given, however, by love and by natural law, with which all reason is filled; out of the books come extravagant and untenable judgments. Let me give you an example of this.

This story is told of Duke Charles of Burgundy. A certain nobleman took an enemy prisoner. The prisoner's wife came to ransom her husband. The nobleman promised to give back the husband on condition that she would lie with him. The woman was virtuous, yet wished to set her husband free; so she goes and asks her husband whether she should do this thing in order to set him free. The husband wished to be set free and to save his life, so he gives his wife permission. After the nobleman had lain with the wife, he had the husband beheaded the next day and gave him to her as a corpse. She laid the whole case before Duke Charles. He summoned the nobleman and commanded him to marry the woman. When the wedding day was over he had the nobleman beheaded, gave the woman possession of his property, and restored her to honor. Thus he punished the crime in a princely way.

Observe: No pope, no jurist, no lawbook could have given him such a decision. It sprang from untrammeled reason, above the law in all the books, and is so excellent that everyone must approve of it and find the justice of it written in his own heart. St. Augustine relates a similar story in *The Lord's Sermon on the Mount*. Therefore, we should keep written laws subject to reason, from which they originally welled forth as from the spring of justice. We should not make the spring dependent on its rivulets, or make reason a captive of letters.

ADMONITION TO PEACE
A REPLY TO
THE TWELVE ARTICLES OF
THE PEASANTS IN SWABIA

1525

Translated by Charles M. Jacobs

Revised by Robert C. Schultz

This open letter was Luther's first response to peasant discontent during 1524–1525 in Swabia, Franconia, and Thuringia. Luther himself had journeyed through Thuringian areas of peasant activity and knew of the attacks on landlords, rulers, monasteries, and churches. Luther hoped by this moderate *Admonition* to achieve some accommodation by the princes of the peasants' demands, and he also wanted to correct and chasten the peasants for their blasphemous use of the gospel and for their violence. Luther had been specifically mentioned in at least two peasant appeals as an appropriate authority for judging the justness of their cause, and this public letter indicates his concern. The text below is from LW 46, 17–43 passim.

The peasants who have now banded together in Swabia have formulated their intolerable grievances against the rulers in twelve articles, and have undertaken to support them with certain passages of Scripture. Now they have published them in printed form. The thing about them that pleases me most is that, in the twelfth article, they offer to accept instruction gladly and willingly, if there is need or necessity for it, and are willing to be corrected, to the extent that it can be done by clear, plain, undeniable passages of Scripture. And it is indeed right and proper that no one's conscience should be instructed or corrected except by Holy Scripture.

* * *

To the Princes and Lords

We have no one on earth to thank for this disastrous rebellion, except you princes and lords, and especially you blind bishops and mad priests and monks, whose hearts are hardened, even to the present day. You do not cease to rant and rave against the holy gospel, even though you know that it is true and that you cannot refute it. In addition, as temporal rulers you do nothing but cheat and rob the people so that you may lead a life of luxury and extravagance. The poor common people cannot bear it any longer. The sword is already at your throats, but you think that you sit so firm in the saddle that no one can unhorse you. This false security and stubborn perversity will break your necks, as you will discover. I have often told you before to beware of the saying, in Psalm 107 [:40], *"Effundit contemptum super principes,"* "He pours contempt upon princes." You, however, keep on asking for trouble and want to be hit over the head. And no warning or exhortation will keep you from getting what you want.

Well, then, since you are the cause of this wrath of God, it will undoubtedly come upon you, unless you mend your ways in time. The signs in heaven and the wonders on earth are meant for you, dear lords; they bode no good for you, and no good will come to you. A great part of God's wrath has already come, for God is sending many false teachers and prophets among us,* so that through our error and blasphemy we may richly deserve hell and everlasting damnation. The rest of it is now here, for the peasants are banding together, and, unless our repentance moves God to prevent it, this must result in the ruin, destruction, and desolation of Germany by cruel murder and bloodshed.

* * *

If it is still possible to give you advice, my lords, give way a little to the will and wrath of God. A cartload of hay must give way to a drunken man —how much more ought you to stop your raging and obstinate tyranny and not deal unreasonably with the peasants, as though they were drunk or out of their minds! Do not start a fight with them, for you do not know how it will end. Try kindness first, for you do not know what God will do to prevent the spark that will kindle all Germany and start a fire that no one can extinguish. Our sins are before God [Ps. 90:8]; therefore we have to fear his wrath when even a leaf rustles [Lev. 26:36], let alone when such a multitude sets itself in motion. You will lose nothing by kindness; and even if you did lose something, the preservation of peace will pay you back ten times. But if there is open conflict you may lose both your property and your life. Why risk danger when you can achieve more by following a different way that is also the better way?

The peasants have just published twelve articles, some of which are so fair and just as to take away your reputation in the eyes of God and the world and fulfil what the Psalm [107:40] says about God pouring contempt upon princes. Nevertheless, almost all of the articles are framed in their own interest and for their own good, though not for their best good. Of course, I would have formulated other articles against you that would have dealt with all Germany and its government.

I did this in my book *To the German Nobility*, when more was at stake; but because you made light of that, you must now listen to and put up with these selfish articles. It serves you right for being a people to whom nothing can be told.

In the first article they ask the right to hear the gospel and choose their pastors. You cannot reject this request with any show of right, even though this article does indeed make some selfish demands, for they allege that these pastors are to be supported by the tithes, and these do not belong to the peasants. Nevertheless, the basic sense of the article is that the preaching of the gospel should be permitted, and no ruler can or ought to oppose this. Indeed, no ruler ought to prevent anyone from teaching or believing what he pleases, whether it is the gospel or lies. It is enough if he prevents the teaching of sedition and rebellion.

The other articles protest economic injustices, such as the death tax. These protests are also right and just, for rulers are not appointed to exploit their subjects for their own profit and advantage, but to be concerned about the welfare of their subjects. And the people cannot tolerate it very long if their rulers set confiscatory tax rates and tax them out of their very skins. What good would it do a peasant if his field bore as many gulden as stalks of wheat if the rulers only taxed him all the more and then wasted it as though

73

it were chaff to increase their luxury, and squandered his money on their own clothes, food, drink, and buildings? Would not the luxury and the extravagant spending have to be checked so that a poor man could keep something for himself? You have undoubtedly received further information from the peasants' tracts, so that you are adequately aware of their grievances.

To the Peasants

So far, dear friends, you have learned only that I agree that it is unfortunately all too true that the princes and lords who forbid the preaching of the gospel and oppress the people unbearably deserve to have God put them down from their thrones [Luke 1:52] because they have sinned so greatly against both God and man. And they have no excuse. Nevertheless, you, too, must be careful that you take up your cause justly and with a good conscience. If you have a good conscience, you have the comforting advantage that God will be with you, and will help you. Even though you did not succeed for a while, or even suffered death, you would win in the end, and you would preserve your souls eternally with all the saints. But if you act unjustly and have a bad conscience, you will be defeated. And even though you might win for a while and even kill all the princes, you would suffer the eternal loss of your body and soul in the end. For you, therefore, this is no laughing matter. The eternal fate of your body and soul is involved. And you must most seriously consider not merely how strong you are and how wrong the princes are, but whether you act justly and with a good conscience.

* * *

In the first place, dear brethren, you bear the name of God and call yourselves a "Christian association" or union, and you allege that you want to live and act according to divine law. Now you know that the name, word, and titles of God are not to be assumed idly or in vain, as he says in the second commandment, "Thou shalt not take the name of the Lord your God in vain," and adds, "for the Lord will not hold him guiltless who takes his name in vain" [Deut. 5:11]. Here is a clear, plain text, which applies to you, as to all men. It threatens you, as well as us and all others, with God's wrath without regard to your great numbers, rights, and terror. God is

74

mighty enough and strong enough to punish you as he here threatens if his name is taken in vain, and you know it. So if you take his name in vain, you may expect no good fortune but only trouble. Learn from this how to judge yourselves and accept this friendly warning. It would be a simple thing for God, who once drowned the whole world with a flood [Gen. 7:17-24] and destroyed Sodom with fire [Gen. 19:24-28], to kill or defeat so many thousands of peasants. He is an almighty and terrible God.

Second, it is easy to prove that you are taking God's name in vain and putting it to shame; nor is there any doubt that you will, in the end, encounter all misfortune, unless God is not true. For here is God's word, spoken through the mouth of Christ, "All who take the sword will perish by the sword" [Matt. 26:52]. That means nothing else than that no one, by his own violence, shall arrogate authority to himself; but as Paul says, "Let every person be subject to the governing authorities with fear and reverence" [Rom. 13:1].

How can you get around these passages and laws of God when you boast that you are acting according to divine law, and yet take the sword in your own hands, and revolt against "the governing authorities that are instituted by God?" Do you think that Paul's judgment in Romans 13 [:2] will not strike you, "He who resists the authorities will incur judgment"? You take God's name in vain when you pretend to be seeking divine right, and under the pretense of his name work contrary to divine right. Be careful, dear sirs. It will not turn out that way in the end.

Third, you say that the rulers are wicked and intolerable, for they will not allow us to have the gospel; they oppress us too hard with the burdens they lay on our property, and they are ruining us in body and soul. I answer: The fact that the rulers are wicked and unjust does not excuse disorder and rebellion, for the punishing of wickedness is not the responsibility of everyone, but of the worldly rulers who bear the sword. Thus Paul says in Romans 13 [:4] and Peter, in I Peter 3 [2:14], that the rulers are instituted by God for the punishment of the wicked. Then, too, there is the natural law of all the world, which says that no one may sit as judge in his own case or take his own revenge. The proverb is true, "Whoever hits back is in the wrong." Or as it is said, "It takes two to start a fight." The divine law agrees with this, and says, in Deuteronomy 32 [:35], "Vengeance is mine; I will repay, says the Lord." Now you cannot deny that your rebellion actually involves you in such a way that you make yourselves your own judges and avenge yourselves. You are quite unwilling to suffer any wrong. That is contrary not only to Christian law and the gospel, but also to natural law and all equity.

* * *

I make you the judges and leave it to you to decide who is the worse robber, the man who takes a large part of another's goods, but leaves him something, or the man who takes everything that he has, and takes his life besides. The rulers unjustly take your property; that is the one side. On the other hand, you take from them their authority, in which their whole property and life and being consist. Therefore you are far greater robbers than they, and you intend to do worse things than they have done. "Indeed not," you say, "We are going to leave them enough to live on." If anyone wants to believe that, let him! I do not believe it. Anyone who dares go so far as to use force to take away authority, which is the main thing, will not stop at that, but will take the other, smaller thing that depends upon it. The wolf that eats a whole sheep will also eat its ear.   And even if you permitted them to keep their life and some property, nevertheless, you would take the best thing they have, namely, their authority, and make yourselves lords over them. That would be too great a robbery and wrong. God will declare you to be the greatest robbers.

Can you not think it through, dear friends? If your enterprise were right, then any man might become judge over another. Then authority, government, law, and order would disappear from the world; there would be nothing but murder and bloodshed. As soon as anyone saw that someone was wronging him, he would begin to judge and punish him. Now if that is unjust and intolerable when done by an individual, we cannot allow a mob or a crowd to do it. However, if we do permit a mob or a crowd to do it, then we cannot rightly and fairly forbid an individual to do it. For in both cases the cause is the same, that is, an injustice. What would you yourselves do if disorder broke out in your ranks and one man set himself against another and took vengeance on him? Would you put up with that? Would you not say that he must let others, whom you appointed, do the judging and avenging? What do you expect God and the world to think when you pass judgment and avenge yourselves on those who have injured you and even upon your rulers, whom God has appointed?

Now in all this I have been speaking of the common, divine, and natural law which even the heathen, Turks, and Jews have to keep if there is to be any peace or order in the world. Even though you were to keep this whole law, you would do no better and no more than the heathen and the Turks do. For no one is a Christian merely because he does not undertake to function as his own judge and avenger but leaves this to the authorities and the rulers.

* * *

And now we want to move on and speak of the law of Christ, and of the gospel, which is not binding on the heathen, as the other law is. For if you claim that you are Christians and like to be called Christians and want to be known as Christians, then you must also allow your law to be held up before you rightly. Listen, then, dear Christians, to your Christian law! Your Supreme Lord Christ, whose name you bear, says, in Matthew 6 [5:39-41], "Do not resist one who is evil. If anyone forces you to go one mile, go with him two miles. If anyone wants to take your coat, let him have your cloak too. If anyone strikes you on one cheek, offer him the other too." Do you hear this, O Christian association? How does your program stand in light of this law? You do not want to endure evil or suffering, but rather want to be free and to experience only goodness and justice. However, Christ says that we should not resist evil or injustice but always yield, suffer, and let things be taken from us. If you will not bear this law, then lay aside the name of Christian and claim another name that accords with your actions, or else Christ himself will tear his name away from you, and that will be too hard for you.

In Romans 12 [:19] Paul says, "Beloved, never avenge yourselves, but leave it to the wrath of God." In this same sense he praises the Corinthians for gladly suffering if someone hits or robs them, II Corinthians 11 [:20]. And in I Corinthians 6 [:1-2] he condemns them for going to court for the sake of property rather than suffering injustice. Indeed, our leader, Jesus Christ, says in Matthew 7 [5:44] that we should bless those who insult us, pray for our persecutors, love our enemies, and do good to those who do evil to us. These, dear friends, are our Christian laws.

Now you can see how far these false prophets have led you astray. They still call you Christians, although they have made you worse than heathen. On the basis of these passages even a child

77

can understand that the Christian law tells us not to strive against injustice, not to grasp the sword, not to protect ourselves, not to avenge ourselves, but to give up life and property, and let whoever takes it have it. We have all we need in our Lord, who will not leave us, as he has promised [Heb. 13:5]. Suffering! suffering! Cross! cross! This and nothing else is the Christian law! But now you are fighting for temporal goods and will not let the coat go after the cloak, but want to recover the cloak. How then will you die and give up your life, or love your enemies and do good to them? O worthless Christians! Dear friends, Christians are not so common-place that so many can assemble in one group. A Christian is a rare bird! Would to God that the majority of us were good, pious heathen, who kept the natural law, not to mention the Christian law!

* * *

In saying this it is not my intention to justify or defend the rulers in the intolerable injustices which you suffer from them. They are unjust, and commit heinous wrongs against you; that I admit. If, however, neither side accepts instruction and you start to fight with each other—may God prevent it!—I hope that neither side will be called Christian. Rather I hope that God will, as is usual in these situations, use one rascal to punish the other. If it comes to a con-flict—may God graciously prevent it!—I hope that your character and name will be so well known that the authorities will recognize that they are fighting not against Christians but against heathen; and that you, too, may know that you are not fighting Christian rulers but heathen. Christians do not fight for themselves with sword and musket, but with the cross and with suffering, just as Christ, our leader, does not bear a sword, but hangs on the cross. Your victory, therefore, does not consist in conquering and reigning, or in the use of force, but in defeat and in weakness, as St. Paul says in II Corinthians 1 [10:4], "The weapons of our warfare are not material, but are the strength which comes from God," and, "Power is made perfect in weakness" [II Cor. 12:9].

Your name and title ought therefore to indicate that you are people who fight because they will not, and ought not, endure in-justice or evil, according to the teaching of nature. You should use that name, and let the name of Christ alone, for that is the kind of works that you are doing. If, however, you will not take that name, but keep the name of Christian, then I must accept the fact that I am also involved in this struggle and consider you as enemies who, under the name of the gospel, act contrary to it, and want to do more to suppress my gospel than anything the pope and emperor have done to suppress it.

* * *

If you were Christians you would stop threatening and resisting with fist and sword. Instead, you would continually abide by the Lord's Prayer and say, "Thy will be done," and, "Deliver us from evil, Amen" [Matt. 6:10, 13]. The psalms show us many examples of genuine saints taking their needs to God and complaining to him about them. They seek help from God: they do not try to defend themselves or to resist evil. That kind of prayer would have been more help to you, in all your needs, than if the world were full of people on your side. This would be especially true if, besides that, you had a good conscience and the comforting assurance that your prayers were heard, as his promises declare: "God is the Savior of all men, especially of those who believe," I Timothy 4 [:10]; "Call upon me in the day of trouble, I will deliver you," Psalm 50 [:15]; "He called upon me in trouble, therefore I will help him," Psalm 91 [:15]. See! That is the Christian way to get rid of misfortune and evil, that is, to endure it and to call upon God. But because you neither call upon God nor patiently endure, but rather help yourselves by your own power and make yourselves your own god and savior, God cannot and must not be your God and Savior. By God's permission you might accomplish something as the heathen and blasphemers you are—and we pray that he will prevent that—but it will only be to your temporal and eternal destruction. However, as Christians, or Evangelicals, you will win nothing. I would stake my life a thousand times on that.

On this basis it is now easy to reply to all your articles. Even though they all were just and equitable in terms of natural law, you have still forgotten the Christian law. You have not been putting this program into effect and achieving your goals by patiently praying to God, as Christians ought to do, but have instead undertaken to compel the rulers to give you what you wanted by using force and violence. This is against the law of the land and against natural justice. The man who composed your articles is no godly and honest man. His marginal notes refer to many chapters of Scripture on which the articles are supposed to be based. But he talks with his mouth full of nothing, and leaves out the passages which would show his own wickedness and that of your cause. He has done this to deceive you, to incite you, and to bring you into danger. Anyone who reads through the chapters cited will realize that they speak very little in favor of what you are doing. On the contrary, they say that men should live and act like Christians. He who seeks to use you to destroy the gospel is a prophet of discord. May God prevent that and guard you against him!

In the preface you are conciliatory and claim that you do not want to be rebels. You even excuse your actions by claiming that you desire to teach and to live according to the gospel. Your own words and actions condemn you. You confess that you are causing disturbances and revolting. And then you try to excuse this behavior with the gospel. You have heard above that the gospel teaches Christians to endure and suffer wrong and to pray to God in every need. You, however, are not willing to suffer, but like heathen, you want to force the rulers to conform to your impatient will. You cite the children of Israel as an example, saying that God heard their crying and delivered them [Exod. 6:5-7]. Why then do you not follow the example that you cite? Call upon God and wait until he sends you a Moses, who will prove by signs and wonders that he is sent from God. The children of Israel did not riot against Pharaoh, or help themselves, as you propose to do. This illustration, therefore, is completely against you, and condemns you. You boast of it, and yet you do the opposite of what it teaches.

Furthermore, your declaration that you teach and live according to the gospel is not true.   Not one of the articles teaches anything of the gospel. Rather, everything is aimed at obtaining freedom for your person and for your property. To sum it up, everything is concerned with worldly and temporal matters. You want power and wealth so that you will not suffer injustice. The gospel, however, does not become involved in the affairs of this world, but speaks of our life in the world in terms of suffering, injustice, the cross, patience, and contempt for this life and temporal wealth.

* * *

It is true, of course, that the rulers may suppress the gospel in cities or places where the gospel is, or where there are preachers; but you can leave these cities or places and follow the gospel to some other place. It is not necessary, for the gospel's sake, for you to capture or occupy the city or place; on the contrary, let the ruler have his city; you follow the gospel. Thus you permit men to wrong you and drive you away; and yet, at the same time, you do not permit men to take the gospel from you or keep it from you. Thus the two things, suffering and not suffering, turn out to be one. If you occupy the city for the sake of the gospel, you rob the ruler of the city of what is his, and pretend that you are doing it for the gospel's sake. Dear friend, the gospel does not teach us to rob or to take things, even though the owner of the property abuses it by using it against God, wrongfully, and to your injury. The gospel needs no physical place or city in which to dwell; it will and must dwell in hearts.

* * *

On the First Article

"The entire community should have the power and authority to choose and appoint a pastor." This article is just only if it is understood in a Christian sense, even though the chapters indicated in the margin do not support it. If the possessions of the parish come from the rulers and not from the community, then the community cannot give these possessions to one whom they choose, for that would be robbery and theft. If they desire a pastor, let them first humbly ask the rulers to give them one. If the rulers are unwilling, then let them choose their own pastor, and support him out of their own possessions; they should let the rulers keep their property, or else secure it from them in a lawful way. But if the rulers will not tolerate the pastor whom they chose and support, then let him flee to another city, and let any flee with him who want to do as Christ teaches. That is a Christian and evangelical way to choose and have one's own pastor. Whoever does otherwise, acts in an un-Christian manner, and is a robber and brawler.

On the Second Article

The pastor "shall receive out of this tithe . . .; the remainder shall be distributed to the poor and needy." This article is nothing but theft and highway robbery. They want to appropriate for themselves the tithes, which are not theirs but the rulers', and want to use them to do what they please. Oh, no, dear friends! That is the same as deposing the rulers altogether. Your preface expressly says that no one is to be deprived of what is his. If you want to give

81

gifts and do good, use your own possessions, as the wise man says [Prov. 3:9]. And God says through Isaiah, "I hate the offering that is given out of stolen goods" [Isa. 61:8]. You speak in this article as though you were already lords in the land and had taken all the property of the rulers for your own and would be no one's subjects, and would give nothing. This shows what your intention really is. Stop it, dear sirs, stop it! It will not be you who puts an end to it! The chapters of Scripture which your lying preacher and false prophet has smeared on the margin do not help you at all; they are against you.

On the Third Article

You assert that no one is to be the serf of anyone else, because Christ has made us all free. That is making Christian freedom a completely physical matter. Did not Abraham [Gen. 17:23] and other patriarchs and prophets have slaves? Read what St. Paul teaches about servants, who, at that time, were all slaves. This article, therefore, absolutely contradicts the gospel. It proposes robbery, for it suggests that every man should take his body away from his lord, even though his body is the lord's property. A slave can be a Christian, and have Christian freedom, in the same way that a prisoner or a sick man is a Christian, and yet not free. This article would make all men equal, and turn the spiritual kingdom of Christ into a worldly, external kingdom; and that is impossible. A worldly kingdom cannot exist without an inequality of persons, some being free, some imprisoned, some lords, some subjects, etc.; and St. Paul says in Galatians 5 that in Christ the lord and the servant are equal.

* * *

On the Other Eight Articles

The other articles, which discuss the freedom to hunt game animals and birds, to catch fish, to use wood from the forest, their obligation to provide free labor, the amount of their rents and taxes, the death tax, etc., are all matters for the lawyers to discuss. It is not fitting that I, an evangelist, should judge or make decisions in such matters. I am to instruct and teach men's consciences in things that concern divine and Christian matters; there are books enough about the other things in the imperial laws. I said above that these things do not concern a Christian, and that he cares nothing about them. He lets anyone who will rob, take, cheat, scrape, devour, and rage—for the Christian is a martyr on earth. Therefore the peasants ought properly to stop using the name Christian and use some other name that would show that they are men who seek their human and natural rights rather than their rights as Christians. For obtaining their rights as Christians would mean they should keep quiet about all these matters and complain only to God when they suffer.

* * *

Admonition to Both Rulers and Peasants

Now, dear sirs, there is nothing Christian on either side and nothing Christian is at issue between you; both lords and peasants are discussing questions of justice and injustice in heathen, or worldly, terms. Furthermore, both parties are acting against God and are under his wrath, as you have heard. For God's sake, then, take my advice! Take a hold of these matters properly, with justice and not with force or violence and do not start endless bloodshed in Germany. For because both of you are wrong, and both of you want to avenge and defend yourselves, both of you will destroy yourselves and God will use one rascal to flog another.

* * *

As I see it, the worst thing about this completely miserable affair is that both sides will sustain irreparable damage; and I would gladly risk my life and even die if I could prevent that from happening. Since neither side fights with a good conscience, but both fight to uphold injustice, it must follow, in the first place, that those who are slain are lost eternally, body and soul, as men who die in their sins, without penitence and without grace, under the wrath of God. Nothing can be done for them. The lords would be fighting to strengthen and maintain their tyranny, their persecution of the gospel, and their unjust oppression of the poor, or else to help that kind of ruler. That is a terrible injustice and is against God. He who commits such a sin must be lost eternally. The peasants, on the other hand, would fight to defend their rebellion and their abuse of the name Christian. Both these things are great sins against God, and he who dies in them or for them must also be lost eternally, and nothing can prevent it.

* * *

I, therefore, sincerely advise you to choose certain counts and lords from among the nobility and certain councilmen from the cities and ask them to arbitrate and settle this dispute amicably. You lords, stop being so stubborn! You will finally have to stop being such oppressive tyrants—whether you want to or not. Give these poor people room in which to live and air to breath. You peasants, let yourselves be instructed and give up the excessive demands of some of your articles. In this way it may be possible to reach a solution of this dispute through human laws and agreements, if not through Christian means.

If you do not follow this advice—God forbid!—I must let you come to blows. But I am innocent of your souls, your blood, or your property. The guilt is yours alone. I have told you that you are both wrong and that what you are fighting for is wrong. You lords are not fighting against Christians—Christians do nothing against you; they prefer to suffer all things—but against outright robbers and defamers of the Christian name. Those of them who die are already condemned eternally. On the other hand, you peasants are not fighting against Christians, but against tyrants, and persecutors of God and man, and murderers of the saints of Christ. Those of them who die are also condemned eternally. There you have God's sure verdict upon both parties. This I know. Do what you please to preserve your bodies and souls, if you will not accept my advice.

I, however, will pray to my God that he will either reconcile you both and bring about an agreement between you, or else graciously prevent things from turning out as you intend. Nonetheless, the terrible signs and wonders that have come to pass in these times give me a heavy heart and make me fear that God's wrath has grown too great; as he says in Jeremiah, "Though Noah, Job, and Daniel stood before me, I would have no pleasure in the people. Would to God that you might fear his wrath and amend your ways that this disaster might be delayed and postponed a while! In any case, my conscience assures me that I have faithfully given you my Christian and fraternal advice. God grant that it helps! Amen.

"His mischief returns upon his own head, and on his own pate his violence descends."

AGAINST THE ROBBING AND MURDERING HORDES OF PEASANTS

1525

Translated by Charles M. Jacobs

Revised by Robert C. Schultz

The *Admonition* was too late to change the course of the peasants' revolt. By early May Luther was convinced that the peasants' blasphemous and chiliastic use of the gospel plus the increasing political violence demanded immediate action. Since preaching had failed, Luther in passionate and harsh language calls on the rulers to attack and break the insurrection. The text below is from *LW* 46, 49–55 passim.

The peasants have taken upon themselves the burden of three terrible sins against God and man; by this they have abundantly merited death in body and soul. In the first place, they have sworn to be true and faithful, submissive and obedient, to their rulers, as Christ commands when he says, "Render to Caesar the things that are Caesar's" [Luke 20:25]. And Romans 13 [:1] says, "Let every person be subject to the governing authorities." Since they are now deliberately and violently breaking this oath of obedience and setting themselves in opposition to their masters, they have forfeited body and soul, as faithless, perjured, lying, disobedient rascals and scoundrels usually do. St. Paul passed this judgment on them in Romans 13 [:2] when he said that those who resist the authorities will bring a judgment upon themselves.

This saying will smite the peasants sooner or later, for God wants people to be loyal and to do their duty.

In the second place, they are starting a rebellion, and are violently robbing and plundering monasteries and castles which are not theirs; by this they have doubly deserved death in body and soul as highwaymen and murderers. Furthermore, anyone who can be proved to be a seditious person is an outlaw before God and the emperor; and whoever is the first to put him to death does right and well. For if a man is in open rebellion, everyone is both his judge and his executioner; just as when a fire starts, the first man who can put it out is the best man to do the job. For rebellion is not just simple murder; it is like a great fire, which attacks and devastates a whole land. Thus rebellion brings with it a land filled with murder and bloodshed; it makes widows and orphans, and turns everything upside down, like the worst disaster. Therefore let everyone who can, smite, slay, and stab, secretly or openly, remembering that nothing can be more poisonous, hurtful, or devilish than a rebel. It is just as when one must kill a mad dog; if you do not strike him, he will strike you, and a whole land with you.

In the third place, they cloak this terrible and horrible sin with the gospel, call themselves "Christian brethren," take oaths and submit to them, and compel people to go along with them in these abominations. Thus they become the worst blasphemers of God and slanderers of his holy name. Under the outward appearance of the gospel, they honor and serve the devil, thus deserving death in body and soul ten times over. I have never heard of a more hideous sin. I suspect that the devil feels that the Last Day is coming and therefore he undertakes such an unheard-of act, as though saying to himself, "This is the end, therefore it shall be the worst; I will stir up the dregs and knock out the bottom." God will guard us against him! See what a mighty prince the devil is, how he has the world in his hands and can throw everything into confusion, when he can so quickly catch so many thousands of peasants, deceive them, blind them, harden them, and throw them into revolt, and do with them whatever his raging fury undertakes.

* * *

Now since the peasants have brought [the wrath of] both God and man down upon themselves and are already many times guilty of death in body and soul, and since they submit to no court and wait for no verdict, but only rage on, I must instruct the temporal authorities on how they may act with a clear conscience in this matter.

First, I will not oppose a ruler who, even though he does not tolerate the gospel, will smite and punish these peasants without first offering to submit the case to judgment.* He is within his rights, since the peasants are not contending any longer for the gospel, but have become faithless, perjured, disobedient, rebellious murderers, robbers, and blasphemers, whom even a heathen ruler has the right and authority to punish. Indeed, it is his duty to punish such scoundrels, for this is why he bears the sword and is "the servant of God to execute his wrath on the wrongdoer," Romans 13 [:4].

But if the ruler is a Christian and tolerates the gospel, so that the peasants have no appearance of a case against him, he should proceed with fear. First he must take the matter to God, confessing that we have deserved these things, and remembering that God may, perhaps, have thus aroused the devil as a punishment upon all Germany. Then he should humbly pray for help against the devil, for we are contending not only "against flesh and blood," but "against the spiritual hosts of wickedness in the air" [Eph. 6:12; 2:2], which must be attacked with prayer. Then, when our hearts are so turned to God that we are ready to let his divine will be done, whether he will or will not have us to be princes and lords, we must go beyond our duty, and offer the mad peasants an opportunity to come to terms, even though they are not worthy of it. Finally, if that does not help, then swiftly take to the sword.

For in this case a prince and lord must remember that according to Romans 13 [:4] he is God's minister and the servant of his wrath and that the sword has been given him to use against such people. If he does not fulfil the duties of his office by punishing some and protecting others, he commits as great a sin before God as when someone who has not been given the sword commits murder. If he is able to punish and does not do it—even though he would have had to kill someone or shed blood—he becomes guilty of all the murder and evil that these people commit. For by deliberately disregarding God's command he permits such rascals to go about their wicked business, even though he was able to prevent it and it was his duty to do so. This is not a time to sleep. And there is no place for patience or mercy. This is the time of the sword, not the day of grace.

* * *

Finally, there is another thing that ought to motivate the rulers. The peasants are not content with belonging to the devil themselves; they force and compel many good people to join their devilish league against their wills, and so make them partakers of all of their own wickedness and damnation. Anyone who consorts with them goes to the devil with them and is guilty of all the evil deeds that they commit, even though he has to do this because he is so weak in faith that he could not resist them. A pious Christian ought to suffer a hundred deaths rather than give a hairsbreadth of consent to the peasants' cause. O how many martyrs could now be made by the bloodthirsty peasants and the prophets of murder! Now the rulers ought to have mercy on these prisoners of the peasants, and if they had no other reason to use the sword with a good conscience against the peasants, and to risk their own lives and property in fighting them, this would be reason enough, and more than enough: they would be rescuing and helping these souls whom the peasants have forced into their devilish league and who, without willing it, are sinning so horribly and must be damned. For truly these souls are in purgatory; indeed, they are in the bonds of hell and the devil.

Therefore, dear lords, here is a place where you can release, rescue, help. Have mercy on these poor people! Let whoever can stab, smite, slay. If you die in doing it, good for you! A more blessed death can never be yours, for you die while obeying the divine word and commandment in Romans 13 [:1, 2], and in loving service of your neighbor, whom you are rescuing from the bonds of hell and of the devil. And so I beg everyone who can to flee from the peasants as from the devil himself; those who do not flee, I pray that God will enlighten and convert. As for those who are not to be converted, God grant that they may have neither fortune nor success. To this let every pious Christian say, "Amen!" For this prayer is right and good, and pleases God; this I know. If anyone thinks this too harsh, let him remember that rebellion is intolerable and that the destruction of the world is to be expected every hour.

AN OPEN LETTER
ON THE HARSH BOOK
AGAINST THE PEASANTS

1525

Translated by Charles M. Jacobs

Revised by Robert C. Schultz

By the end of May, 1525, the peasants' revolt had been crushed, and the rulers were taking their revenge. In the aftermath of the princes' bloodbath against the defeated peasants, Luther came under severe criticism by friend and foe alike. It was said that Luther's second tract, *Against the Robbing and Murdering Hordes of Peasants*, justified the cruel and vengeful acts of the rulers, that he had deserted the peasants even though through his writings he had had some hand in encouraging them, that he had become a flatterer of princes, and that there was an inconsistency between the moderate *Admonition* and the harsh and brutal second tract. After much urging, Luther finally published a reply in August, 1525. The text below is from *LW* 46, 63–85 passim.

To the honorable and wise Caspar Müller, chancellor of Mansfeld, my good friend. Grace and peace in Christ.

I have been obliged to answer your letter in a printed book because the little book that I published against the peasants has given rise to so many complaints and questions, as though it were un-Christian and too hard. Indeed, I had intended to plug my ears and to let those blind, ungrateful creatures who seek nothing in me but causes of offense smother in their own vexation until they had to rot in it. It seems that reading my other books has not helped men to accept such a plain, simple judgment about earthly things. For I remembered the word of Christ in John 3 [:12], "If I have told you earthly things and you do not believe, how can you believe if I tell you heavenly things?" And when the disciples asked, "Do you know that the Pharisees were offended when they heard this saying?" he said, "Let them be offended. They are blind and blind leaders of the blind," Matthew 15 [:12-14].

They cry and boast, "There, there you see Luther's spirit! He teaches bloodshed without any mercy. The devil must speak through him." Oh, well, if I were not used to being judged and condemned, I might become excited; but nothing makes me prouder than when my work and teaching suffers reverses and is crucified. No one is satisfied unless he can condemn Luther. Luther is the target of opposition. Everyone has to win his spurs against him and carry off the honors of the tournament. In these matters everyone else has a higher spirit than I, and I must be altogether fleshly. Would to God that they had a higher spirit! Indeed, I would gladly be a man of flesh and say, as St. Paul said to his Corinthians, "You are rich. You are full. You rule without us" [I Cor. 4:8]. But I fear it is all too true that they have a high spirit, for I have not as yet seen them undertake very much that does not bring them to sin and shame.

* * *

First of all, then, I must warn those who criticize my book to hold their tongues and to be careful not to make a mistake and lose their own heads; for they are certainly rebels at heart, and Solomon says, "My son, fear the Lord and the king, and do not be a fellow-traveler with the rebels for their disaster will come suddenly and who can know what the ruin of both you and them will be?" Proverbs 24 [:21-22]. Thus we see that both rebels and those who join them are condemned. God does not want us to make a joke out of this but to fear the king and the government. Those who are fellow-travelers with rebels sympathize with them, feel sorry for them, justify them, and show mercy to those on whom God has no mercy, but whom he wishes to have punished and destroyed. For the man who thus sympathizes with the rebels makes it perfectly clear that he has decided in his heart that he will also cause disaster if he has the opportunity. The rulers, therefore, ought to shake these people up until they keep their mouths shut and realize that the rulers are serious.

If they think this answer is too harsh, and that this is talking violence and only shutting men's mouths, I reply, "That is right." A rebel is not worth rational arguments, for he does not accept them. You have to answer people like that with a fist, until the sweat drips off their noses. The peasants would not listen; they would not let anyone tell them anything, so their ears must now be unbuttoned with musket balls till their heads jump off their shoulders. Such pupils need such a rod. He who will not hear God's word when it is spoken with kindness, must listen to the headsman, when he comes with his axe. If anyone says that I am being uncharitable and unmerciful about this, my reply is: This is not a question of mercy; we are talking of God's word. It is God's will that the king be honored and the rebels destroyed; and he is as merciful as we are.

* * *

And yet, in order that the righteous God may hold his own against these his judges, and that his decree be found just and pure, we shall undertake to advocate his word against these blasphemers and show the reason for his divine will, and light two candles for the devil. They cast it up to me that Christ teaches, "Be merciful, even as your Father is merciful" [Luke 6:36]; and again, "I desire mercy and not sacrifice" [Matt. 9:13]; and again, "The Son of man is come not to destroy souls, but to save them" [Luke 19:10], etc. And they think this hits the nail on the head. "Luther ought to have taught that we should have mercy on the peasants, and he teaches, instead, that we should kill them immediately. What do you think of that? Let us see whether Luther will get out of this! I think he is caught." Well now, I thank you, dear teachers. If these lofty spirits had not taught me, how would I ever have known this or found it out? How should I know that God demands mercy —I, who have taught and written more about mercy than any other man in a thousand years?

It is the very devil himself who wants to do all the evil that he can, and so he stirs up good and pious hearts and tempts them with things like this, so that they may not see how black he is, and he tries to deck himself out in a reputation for mercy. But it will not help him! My good friends, you praise mercy so highly because the peasants are beaten; why did you not praise it when the peasants were raging, smiting, robbing, burning, and plundering, in ways that are terrible to see or even to hear about? Why were they not merciful to the princes and lords, whom they wanted to exterminate completely? No one spoke of mercy then. Everything was "rights"; nothing was said of mercy, it was nothing. "Rights, rights, rights!" They were everything. Now that the peasants are beaten, and the stone that they threw at heaven is falling back on their own heads, no one is to say anything of rights, but to speak only of mercy.

* * *

So much for the un-Christian and merciless bloodhounds who praise the sayings about mercy so that sheer wickedness and mercilessness may rule in the world as they please! To the others, whom they have led astray, or who are so weak that they cannot reconcile my book with the words of Christ, I have this to say: There are two kingdoms, one the kingdom of God, the other the kingdom of the world. I have written this so often that I am surprised that there is anyone who does not know it or remember it. Anyone who knows how to distinguish rightly between these two kingdoms will certainly not be offended by my little book, and he will also properly understand the passages about mercy. God's kingdom is a kingdom of grace and mercy, not of wrath and punishment. In it there is only forgiveness, consideration for one another, love, service, the doing of good, peace, joy, etc. But the kingdom of the world is a kingdom of wrath and severity. In it there is only punishment, repression, judgment, and condemnation to restrain the wicked and protect the good. For this reason it has the sword, and Scripture calls a prince or lord "God's wrath," or "God's rod" (Isaiah 14 [:5-6]).

The Scripture passages which speak of mercy apply to the kingdom of God and to Christians, not to the kingdom of the world, for it is a Christian's duty not only to be merciful, but also to endure every kind of suffering—robbery, arson, murder, devil, and hell. It goes without saying that he is not to strike, kill, or take revenge on anyone. But the kingdom of the world, which is nothing else than the servant of God's wrath upon the wicked and is a real precursor of hell and everlasting death, should not be merciful, but strict, severe, and wrathful in fulfilling its work and duty. Its tool is not a wreath of roses or a flower of love, but a naked sword; and a sword is a symbol of wrath, severity, and punishment. It is turned only against the wicked, to hold them in check and keep them at peace, and to protect and save the righteous [Rom. 13:3-4]. Therefore God decrees, in the law of Moses and in Exodus 22 [21:14] where he institutes the sword, "You shall take the murderer from my altar, and not have mercy on him." And the Epistle to the Hebrews [10:28] acknowledges that he who violates the law must die without mercy. This shows that in the exercise of their office, worldly rulers cannot and ought not be merciful—though out of grace, they may take a day off from their office.

Now he who would confuse these two kingdoms—as our false fanatics do—would put wrath into God's kingdom and mercy into the world's kingdom; and that is the same as putting the devil in heaven and God in hell. These sympathizers with the peasants would like to do both of these things. First they wanted to go to work with the sword, fight for the gospel as "Christian brethren," and kill other people, who were supposed to be merciful and patient. Now that the kingdom of the world has overcome them, they want to have mercy in it; that is to say, they are unwilling to endure the worldly kingdom, but will not grant God's kingdom to anyone. Can you imagine anything more perverse? Not so, dear friends! If one has deserved wrath in the kingdom of the world, let him submit, and either take his punishment, or humbly sue for pardon. Those who are in God's kingdom ought to have mercy on everyone and pray for everyone, and yet not hinder the kingdom of the world in the maintenance of its laws and the performance of its duty; rather they should assist it.

Although the severity and wrath of the world's kingdom seems unmerciful, nevertheless, when we see it rightly, it is not the least of God's mercies. Let everyone consider and decide the following case. Suppose I had a wife and children, a house, servants, and property, and a thief or murderer fell upon me, killed me in my own house, ravished my wife and children, took all that I had, and went unpunished so that he could do the same thing again, when he wished. Tell me, who would be more in need of mercy in such a case, I or the thief and murderer? Without doubt it would be I who would need most that people should have mercy on me. But how can this mercy be shown to me and my poor, miserable wife and children, except by restraining such a scoundrel, and by protecting me and maintaining my rights, or, if he will not be restrained and keeps it up, by giving him what he deserves and punishing him, so that he must stop it? What a fine mercy to me it would be, to have mercy on the thief and murderer, and let him kill, abuse, and rob me!

These advocates of the peasants do not consider this kind of mercy which rules and acts through the temporal sword. They see and talk only about the wrath and say that we are flattering the furious princes and lords when we teach that they are to punish the wicked. And yet they are themselves ten times worse flatterers of the murderous scoundrels and wicked peasants. Indeed, they are bloodthirsty murderers, rebels at heart, for they have no mercy on those whom the peasants overthrew, robbed, dishonored, and subjected to all kinds of injustice. For if the intentions of the peasants had been carried out, no honest man would have been safe from them, but whoever had one cent more than another would have had to suffer for it. They had already begun that, and it would not have stopped there; women and children would have been put to shame; they would have taken to killing each other, too, and there would have been no peace or safety anywhere. Has anything ever been heard of that is more unrestrained than a mob of peasants when they are filled with food and have got power? As Solomon says, in Proverbs 30 [:21-22], "Such people the world cannot bear."

* * *

"Not at all," they say. "We are not talking about the obdurate peasants who are unwilling to surrender, but of those who have been defeated or have surrendered. The princes ought to show them mercy, and not treat them so cruelly." I answer: You cannot be a good man if you slander my little book and say that in it I speak of such conquered peasants, or of those who have surrendered; I made it plain that I was speaking of those who were first approached in a friendly way, and would not respond. All my words were directed against the obdurate, hardened, blinded peasants, who would neither see nor hear, as anyone may see who reads them; and yet you say that I advocate the merciless slaughter of the poor captured peasants. If you are going to read books this way and interpret them as you please, what book will have any chance with you? Therefore, as I wrote then so I write now: Let no one have mercy on the obstinate, hardened, blinded peasants who refuse to listen to reason; but let everyone, as he is able, strike, hew, stab, and slay, as though among mad dogs, so that by so doing he may show mercy to those who are ruined, put to flight, and led astray by these peasants, so that peace and safety may be maintained. It is better to cut off one member without mercy than to have the whole body perish by fire, or by disease [Matt. 5:29-30]. How do you like that? Am I still a preacher of the gospel who advocates grace and mercy? If you think I am not, it makes little difference, for you are a bloodhound, and a rebellious murderer and destroyer of the country, you and your rebellious peasants, whom you are flattering in their rebellion.

They say further that the peasants have slain no one in the way they themselves are being slain. What shall be said to that? What a splendid argument! They have slain no one! That was because people had to do what they wanted! They threatened to kill those who would not go along with them; they laid hold of the sword that did not belong to them; they attacked property, houses, and possessions. Arguing this way, a thief and murderer who took from me what he wanted by threatening to kill me would be no murderer. If they had done what they were asked in a kind way to do, they would not have been killed; but because they were not willing to do it, it was right to do to them what they themselves had done or threatened to do to those who did not agree with them. Besides, it is plain that they are faithless, perjured, disobedient, rebellious thieves, robbers, murderers, and blasphemers, and there is not one of them who has not deserved to be put to death ten times without mercy. People are not seeing straight in the matter. They see only the punishment and the pain and not the crime and its guilt and the indescribable injury and ruin that would have resulted. If the punishment hurts, stop doing evil. Paul gives the same answer to this kind of people when he says in Romans 13 [:3-4], "Would you have no fear of him who is in authority? Then do what is good. . . . But if you do evil, be afraid."

They say, in the third place, that the lords are misusing their sword and slaying too cruelly. I answer: What has that to do with my book? Why lay others' guilt on me? If they are misusing their power, they have not learned it from me; and they will have their reward. For the Supreme Judge, who is using them to punish the self-willed peasants, has not forgotten them either, and they will not escape him. My book speaks not of what the lords deserve, but of what the peasants deserve and how they ought to be punished; I have deceived no one about that. When I have time and occasion to do so, I shall attack the princes and lords, too, for in my office of teacher, a prince is the same to me as a peasant. I have already served them faithfully in ways that have not made me very popular with them; but I do not care about that. I have One who is greater than all of them, as St. John [Matt. 3:11] says.

* * *

If you want to live in a community, you must share the community's burdens, dangers, and injuries, even though not you, but your neighbor has caused them. You must do this in the same way that you enjoy the peace, profit, protection, wealth, freedom, and security of the community, even though you have not won them or brought them into being. You must learn to take comfort and sing with Job, "Shall we receive good at the hand of the Lord, and shall we not also receive evil?" [Job 2:10]. So many good days are worth a bad hour, and so many good years are worth a bad day, or year. For a long time we have had peace and good times, until we became presumptuous and self-confident, did not know what peace and good days meant, and did not once thank God for them; now we have to learn.

My advice is to stop complaining and murmuring and thank God that, by his grace and mercy, we have not experienced the greater misfortune which the devil intended to bring upon us through the peasants. That is what Jeremiah did when the Jews were driven out and captured and slain. He comforted himself and said, "It is of the Lord's grace and goodness that we are not entirely destroyed." We Germans are much worse than the Jews, and yet we have not been driven out and slain, as they were; but we want to murmur and become impatient and justify ourselves. We are so unwilling to have a part of us slain that God's wrath against us may increase and he may let us go to destruction, remove his hand, and give us over entirely to the devil. We are acting as we mad Germans always do: we know nothing about God, and we talk about these things as though there were no God who does them and wills that they be done. We do not intend to suffer at all, but to be nobles, who can sit on cushions and do as they please.

You would really have seen something if this devil's business of the peasants had gone on and if God had not answered the prayers of godly Christians and restrained them with the sword. Throughout all Germany, people would have suffered exactly what those suffer who are now being killed and destroyed; only it would have been much worse. No one would have been safe from another; any man might have killed another, burned down his house and barn, and abused his wife and children. For this business did not start with God: there was no order in it; they had already reached the state where no one trusted or believed the other; they deposed one captain after another; and things were done, not as honest men would have had them done, but according to the wishes of the vilest scoundrels. The devil intended to lay all Germany to utter waste because there was no other way by which he could suppress the gospel. Who knows what will yet happen, if we keep on with our murmuring and ingratitude? God can let the peasants go mad again, or release some other plague upon us, so that things may become worse than they are now. I think that this has been a good strong warning and threat. If we disregard it, and neither repent nor fear God, let us beware of what may come to us, lest this shall prove to have been only a joke, and a really serious situation confronts us in the future.

Finally it may be said, "You yourself teach rebellion, for you say that everyone who can, should hew and stab among the rebels, and that, in this case, everyone is both supreme judge and executioner." I reply: My little book was not written against ordinary evildoers, but against rebels. You must make a very, very great distinction between a rebel and a thief, or a murderer, or any other kind of evildoer. A murderer or evildoer lets the head of the government alone and attacks only the members or their property; indeed, he fears the ruler. So long as the head remains, no one ought to attack such a murderer, because the head can punish. Everyone ought to await the judgment and command of the head, to whom God has committed the sword and the office of punishment. But a rebel attacks the head himself and interferes with the exercise of his sword and his office, and therefore his crime is not to be compared with that of a murderer. We cannot wait until the head gives commands and passes judgment, for the head himself is captured and beaten and cannot give them. Rather, everyone who can must run, uncalled and unbidden, and, as a true member, help to rescue his head by stabbing, hewing, and killing, and risk his life and goods for the sake of the head.

* * *

I am called a clergyman and am a minister of the word, but even if I served a Turk and saw my lord in danger, I would forget my spiritual office and stab and hew as long as my heart beat. If I were slain in so doing, I should go straight to heaven. For rebellion is a crime that deserves neither a court trial nor mercy, whether it be among heathen, Jews, Turks, Christians, or any other people; the rebel has already been tried, judged, condemned, and sentenced to death and everyone is authorized to execute him. Nothing more needs to be done than to give him his due and to execute him. No murderer does so much evil, and none deserves so much evil. For a murderer commits a punishable offense, and lets the penalty stand; but a rebel tries to make wickedness free and unpunishable, and attacks the punishment itself. Moreover, he now gives the gospel a bad reputation with its enemies, who blame the gospel for this rebellion and open their slanderous mouths wide enough in blaspheming against it, although this does not excuse them and they know better. Christ will smite them, too, in his own time.

See, then, if I was not right when I said in my little book that we ought to slay the rebels without any mercy. I did not teach, however, that mercy ought not be shown to the captives and those who have surrendered. They accuse me of having said it, but my book proves the opposite. Nor do I intend here to strengthen the raging tyrants, or to praise their raving, for I hear that some of my "knightlets" are treating the poor people with unbounded cruelty, and are very bold and defiant, as though they had won the victory and were firmly in the saddle. They are not seeking to punish and stop the rebellion; rather are they satisfying their furious self-will and cooling a rage which they, perhaps, have long nursed, thinking that they now have an opportunity and excuse to do so. And they are also devoting more energy to their opposition of the gospel; they are trying to re-establish the monasteries and endowed ecclesiastical foundations. And to preserve the pope's crown, they deliberately confuse our cause with that of the rebels. But soon they will reap what they are now sowing [Gal. 6:7]. He who sits in heaven sees them, and he will come before they expect him. Their plans will fail, as they have failed before; this I know.

* * *

I earnestly ask you, and everyone, to read my book fairly, and not run through it so hurriedly. Then you will see that I was advising only Christian and pious rulers, as befits a Christian preacher. I say it again and for the third time. I was writing only for rulers who might wish to deal in a Christian or otherwise honest way with their people, to instruct their consciences concerning this matter to the effect that they ought to take immediate action against the bands of rebels both innocent and guilty. And if they struck the innocent, they were not to let their consciences trouble them, since they were by the very act confessing that they were bound to do their duty to God. Afterward, however, if they won, they were to show grace, not only to those whom they considered innocent, but to the guilty as well.

But these furious, raving, senseless tyrants, who even after the battle cannot get their fill of blood, and in all their lives ask scarcely a question about Christ—these I did not undertake to instruct. It makes no difference to these bloody dogs whether they slay the guilty or the innocent, whether they please God or the devil. They have the sword, but they use it to vent their lust and self-will. I leave them to the guidance of their master, the devil, who is indeed leading them. I have heard that at Mühlhausen one of these big shots summoned the poor wife of Thomas Münzer, now a pregnant widow, fell on one knee before her, and said, "Dear lady, let me ° ° ° you." O a knightly, noble deed, done to a poor, helpless, pregnant little woman! That is a brave hero for you! He is worth three knights, at the very least! Why should I write for scoundrels and hogs like that? The Scriptures call such people "beasts" [Titus 1:12], that is, "wild animals," such as wolves, boars, bears, and lions, and I shall not make men of them; and yet we must put up with them, when God plagues us with them. I had two fears. If the peasants became lords, the devil would become abbot; but if these tyrants became lords, the devil's mother would become abbess. Therefore I wanted to do two things: quiet the peasants, and instruct the pious lords. The peasants were unwilling to listen, and now they have their reward; the lords, too, will not hear, and they shall have their reward also. However, it would have been a shame if they had been killed by the peasants; that would have been too easy a punishment for them. Hell-fire, trembling, and gnashing of teeth [Matt. 22:13] in hell will be their reward eternally, unless they repent.

WHETHER SOLDIERS, TOO, CAN BE SAVED

1526

Translated by Charles M. Jacobs

Revised by Robert C. Schultz

This tract was published by Luther in late December, 1526, following the requests of several professional soldiers who asked for religious guidance. The Christian's attitude toward war had become an immediate practical problem. In March, 1526, the Catholic Emperor Charles V had called for all Catholic rulers to suppress the Lutheran heretics, and an alliance of Catholic princes had been formed for that purpose. The Protestant rulers had responded by forming their own alliance. In addition to the real threat of a religious war within Christendom, the Turks were threatening Europe as a result of their August, 1526, victories in Bohemia and Hungary. Luther explains how a soldier can fulfill his Christian obligations in warfare. The text below is from *LW* 46, 93–137 passim.

In the first place, we must distinguish between an occupation and the man who holds it, between a work and the man who does it. An occupation or a work can be good and right in itself and yet be bad and wrong if the man who does the work is evil or wrong or does not do his work properly. The occupation of a judge is a valuable divine office. This is true both of the office of the trial judge who declares the verdict and the executioner who carries out the sentence. But when the office is assumed by one to whom it has not been committed or when one who holds it rightly uses it to gain riches or popularity, then it is no longer right or good. The married state is also precious and godly, but there are many rascals and scoundrels in it. It is the same way with the profession

64946

or work of the soldier; in itself it is right and godly, but we must see to it that the persons who are in this profession and who do the work are the right kind of persons, that is, godly and upright, as we shall hear.

In the second place, I want you to understand that here I am not speaking about the righteousness that makes men good in the sight of God. Only faith in Jesus Christ can do that; and it is granted and given us by the grace of God alone, without any works or merits of our own, as I have written and taught so often and so much in other places. Rather, I am speaking here about external righteousness which is to be sought in offices and works. In other words, to put it plainly, I am dealing here with such questions as these: whether the Christian faith, by which we are accounted righteous before God, is compatible with being a soldier, going to war, stabbing and killing, robbing and burning, as military law requires us to do to our enemies in wartime. Is this work sinful or unjust? Should it give us a bad conscience before God? Must a Christian only do good and love, and kill no one, nor do anyone any harm? I say that this office or work, even though it is godly and right, can nevertheless become evil and unjust if the person engaged in it is evil and unjust.

In the third place, it is not my intention to explain here at length how the occupation and work of a soldier is in itself right and godly because I have written quite enough about that in my book *Temporal Authority: To What Extent It Should Be Obeyed.* Indeed, I might boast here that not since the time of the apostles have the temporal sword and temporal government been so clearly described or so highly praised as by me. Even my enemies must admit this, but the reward, honor, and thanks that I have earned by it are to have my doctrine called seditious and condemned as resistance to rulers. God be praised for that! For the very fact that the sword has been instituted by God to punish the evil, protect the good, and preserve peace [Rom. 13:1-4; I Pet. 2:13-14] is powerful and sufficient proof that war and killing along with all the things that accompany wartime and martial law have been instituted by God. What else is war but the punishment of wrong and evil? Why does anyone go to war, except because he desires peace and obedience?

Now slaying and robbing do not seem to be works of love. A simple man therefore does not think it is a Christian thing to do.

In truth, however, even this is a work of love. For example, a good doctor sometimes finds so serious and terrible a sickness that he must amputate or destroy a hand, foot, ear, eye, to save the body. Looking at it from the point of view of the organ that he amputates, he appears to be a cruel and merciless man; but looking at it from the point of view of the body, which the doctor wants to save, he is a fine and true man and does a good and Christian work, as far as the work itself is concerned. In the same way, when I think of a soldier fulfilling his office by punishing the wicked, killing the wicked, and creating so much misery, it seems an un-Christian work completely contrary to Christian love. But when I think of how it protects the good and keeps and preserves wife and child, house and farm, property, and honor and peace, then I see how precious and godly this work is; and I observe that it amputates a leg or a hand, so that the whole body may not perish. For if the sword were not on guard to preserve peace, everything in the world would be ruined because of lack of peace. Therefore, such a war is only a very brief lack of peace that prevents an everlasting and immeasurable lack of peace, a small misfortune that prevents a great misfortune.

What men write about war, saying that it is a great plague, is all true. But they should also consider how great the plague is that war prevents. If people were good and wanted to keep peace, war would be the greatest plague on earth. But what are you going to do about the fact that people will not keep the peace, but rob, steal, kill, outrage women and children, and take away property and honor? The small lack of peace called war or the sword must set a limit to this universal, worldwide lack of peace which would destroy everyone.

This is why God honors the sword so highly that he says that he himself has instituted it [Rom. 13:1] and does not want men to say or think that they have invented it or instituted it. For the hand that wields this sword and kills with it is not man's hand, but God's; and it is not man, but God, who hangs, tortures, beheads, kills, and fights. All these are God's works and judgments.

To sum it up, we must, in thinking about a soldier's office, not concentrate on the killing, burning, striking, hitting, seizing, etc. This is what children with their limited and restricted vision see when they regard a doctor as a sawbones who amputates, but do not see that he does this only to save the whole body. So, too, we must look at the office of the soldier, or the sword, with the eyes of an adult and see why this office slays and acts so cruelly. Then it will prove itself to be an office which, in itself, is godly and as needful and useful to the world as eating and drinking or any other work.

* * *

Just think now! If we gave in on this point and admitted that war was wrong in itself, then we would have to give in on all other points and allow that the use of the sword was entirely wrong. For if it is wrong to use a sword in war, it is also wrong to use a sword to punish evildoers or to keep the peace. Briefly, every use of the sword would have to be wrong. For what is just war but the punishment of evildoers and the maintenance of peace? If one punishes a thief or a murderer or an adulterer, that is punishment inflicted on a single evildoer; but in a just war a whole crowd of evildoers, who are doing harm in proportion to the size of the crowd, are punished at once. If, therefore, one work of the sword is good and right, they are all good and right, for the sword is a sword and not a foxtail with which to tickle people. Romans 13 [:4] calls the sword "the wrath of God."

As for the objection that Christians have not been commanded to fight and that these examples are not enough, especially because Christ teaches us not to resist evil but rather suffer all things [Matt. 5:39-42], I have already said all that needs to be said on this matter in my book *Temporal Authority*. Indeed, Christians do not fight and have no worldly rulers among them. Their government is a spiritual government, and, according to the Spirit, they are subjects of no one but Christ. Nevertheless, as far as body and property are concerned, they are subject to worldly rulers and owe them obedience. If worldly rulers call upon them to fight, then they ought to and must fight and be obedient, not as Christians, but as members of the state and obedient subjects. Christians therefore do not fight as individuals or for their own benefit, but as obedient servants of the authorities under whom they live. This is what St. Paul wrote to Titus when he said that Christians should obey the authorities [Titus 3:1]. You may read more about this in my book *Temporal Authority*.

That is the sum and substance of it. The office of the sword is in itself right and is a divine and useful ordinance, which God does not want us to despise, but to fear, honor, and obey, under penalty of punishment, as St. Paul says in Romans 13 [:1-5]. For God has established two kinds of government among men. The one is spiritual; it has no sword, but it has the word, by means of which men are to become good and righteous, so that with this righteousness they may attain eternal life. He administers this righteousness through the word, which he has committed to the preachers. The other kind is worldly government, which works through the sword so that those who do not want to be good and righteous to eternal life may be forced to become good and righteous in the eyes of the world. He administers this righteousness through the sword. And although God will not reward this kind of righteousness with eternal life, nonetheless, he still wishes peace to be maintained among men and rewards them with temporal blessings. He gives rulers much more property, honor, and power than he gives to others so that they may serve him by administering this temporal righteousness. Thus God himself is the founder, lord, master, protector, and rewarder of both kinds of righteousness. There is no human ordinance or authority in either, but each is a divine thing entirely.

Since, then, there is no doubt that the military profession is in itself a legitimate and godly calling and occupation, we will now discuss the persons who are in it and the use they make of their position, for it is most important to know who is to use this office and how he is to use it. And here we have to face the fact that it is impossible to establish hard and fast rules and laws in this matter. There are so many cases and so many exceptions to any rule that it is very difficult or even impossible to decide everything accurately and equitably. This is true of all laws; they can never be formulated so certainly and so justly that cases do not arise which deserve to be made exceptions. If we do not make exceptions and strictly follow the law we do the greatest injustice of all, as the heathen author Terence has said, "The strictest law is the greatest injustice." And Solomon teaches in Ecclesiastes [7:16; 10:1] that we should not carry justice to an extreme and at times should not seek to be wise.

Let me give an example. In the recent rebellion of the peasants there were some who were involved against their will. These were especially people who were well-to-do, for the rebellion struck at the rich, as well as the rulers, and it may fairly be assumed that no rich man favored the rebellion. In any case, some were involved against their will. Some yielded under this pressure, thinking that they could restrain this mad mob and that their good advice would, to some extent, prevent the peasants from carrying out their evil purpose and doing so much evil. They thought that they would be doing both themselves and the authorities a service. Still others became involved with the prior consent and approval of their lords, whom they consulted in advance. There may have been other similar cases.   For no one can imagine all of them, or take them all into account in the law.

Here is what the law says, "All rebels deserve death, and these three kinds of men were apprehended among the rebellious crowd, in the very act of rebellion." What shall we do to them? If we allow no exceptions and let the law take its strict course, they must die just like the others, who are guilty of deliberate and intentional rebellion, although some of the men of whom we speak were innocent in their hearts and honestly tried to serve the authorities. Some of our knightlets, however, refused to make such exceptions, especially if the man involved was rich. They thought they could take their property by saying, "You also were in the mob. You must die." In this way they have committed a great injustice to many people and shed innocent blood, made widows and orphans, and taken their property besides.   And yet they call themselves "nobles." Nobles indeed! The excrement of the eagle can boast that it comes from the eagle's body even though it stinks and is useless; and so these men can also be of the nobility.   We Germans are and remain Germans, that is, swine and senseless beasts.

Now I say that in cases like the three kinds mentioned above, the law ought to yield and justice take its place. For the law matter of factly says, "Rebellion is punishable with death; it is the *crimen lese maiestatis,* a sin against the rulers."   But justice says, "Yes, dear law, it is as you say; but it can happen that two men do similar acts with differing motives in their hearts. Judas, for example, kissed Christ in the garden. Outwardly this was a good work; but his heart was evil and he used a good work, which Christ and his disciples at other times did for one another with good hearts, to betray his Lord [Matt. 26:49]. Here is another example: Peter sat down by the fire with the servants of Annas and warmed himself with the godless, and that was not good

[Luke 22:55]. Now if we were to apply the law strictly, Judas would have to be a good man and Peter a rascal; but Judas' heart was evil and Peter's was good; therefore justice in this case must correct the law.

* * *

In Greek this virtue, or wisdom, which can and must guide and moderate the severity of law according to cases, and which judges the same deed to be good or evil according to the difference of the motives and intentions of the heart, is called *epieikeia;* in Latin it is *aequitas,* and *Billichkeit* in German. Now because law must be framed simply and briefly, it cannot possibly embrace all the cases and problems. This is why the judges and lords must be wise and pious in this matter and mete out reasonable justice, and let the law take its course, or set it aside, accordingly. The head of a household makes a law for his servants, telling them what they are to do on this day or that; that is the law, and the servant who does not keep it must take his punishment. But now one of them may be sick, or be otherwise hindered from keeping the law through no fault of his own; then the law is suspended, and anyone who would punish his servant for that kind of neglect of duty would have to be a mad lord of the house. Similarly, all laws that regulate men's actions must be subject to justice, their mistress, because of the innumerable and varied circumstances which no one can anticipate or set down.

So then, we have this to say about people who live under military law or who are involved in fighting a war. First, war may be made by three kinds of people. An equal may make war against his equal, that is, neither of the two persons is the vassal or subject of the other even though one may be less great or glorious or mighty than the other. Or an overlord may fight against his subject. Or a subject may fight against his overlord. Let us take the third case. Here is what the law says, "No one shall fight or make war against his overlord; for a man owes his overlord obedience, honor, and fear" (Romans 13 [:1-7]). If you chop over your head, the chips fall in your eyes. And Solomon says, "If you throw a stone into the air, it will land on your own head." That is the law in a nutshell. God himself has instituted it and men have accepted it, for it is not possible both to obey and resist, to be subject and not put up with their lords.

But we have already said that justice ought to be the mistress of law, and where circumstances demand it, guide the law, or even command and permit men to act against it. Therefore the question here is whether a situation can ever develop in which it is just for people to act against this law, to be disobedient to rulers and fight against them, depose them, or put them in bonds.

* * *

My reason for saying this is that God says, "Vengeance is mine, I will repay" [Rom. 12:19]. He also says, "Judge not" [Matt. 7:1]. And the Old Testament strictly and frequently forbids cursing rulers or speaking evil about them. Exodus 23 [22:28] says, "You shall not curse the prince of your people." Paul, in I Timothy 2 [:1-2], teaches Christians to pray for their rulers, etc. Solomon in Proverbs and Ecclesiastes repeatedly teaches us to obey the king and be subject to him. Now no one can deny that when subjects set themselves against their rulers, they avenge themselves and make themselves judges. This is not only against the ordinance and command of God, who reserves to himself the authority to pass judgment and administer punishment in these matters, but such actions are also contrary to all natural law and justice. This is the meaning of the proverbs, "No man ought to judge his own case," and, "The man who hits back is in the wrong."

Now perhaps you will say, "How can anyone possibly endure all the injustice that these tyrants inflict on us? You allow them too much opportunity to be unjust, and thus your teaching only makes them worse and worse. Are we supposed to permit everyone's wife and child, body and property to be so shamefully treated and always to be in danger? If we have to live under these conditions, how can we ever begin to live a decent life?" My reply is this: My teaching is not intended for people like you who want to do whatever you think is good and will please you. Go ahead! Do whatever you want! Kill all your lords! See what good is does you! My teaching is intended only for those who would like to do what is right. To these I say that rulers are not to be opposed with violence and rebellion, as the Romans, the Greeks, the Swiss, and the Danes have done; rather, there are other ways of dealing with them.

In the first place, if you see that the rulers think so little of their soul's salvation that they rage and do wrong, what does it matter to you if they ruin your property, body, wife, and child? They cannot hurt your soul, and they do themselves more harm than they do you because they damn their own souls and that must result in the ruin of body and property. Do you think that you are not already sufficiently avenged?

In the second place, what would you do if your rulers were at war and not only your goods and wives and children, but you yourself were broken, imprisoned, burned, and killed for your lord's sake? Would you slay your lord for that reason? Think of all the good people that Emperor Maximilian lost in the wars that he waged in his lifetime. No one did anything to him because of it. And yet, if he had destroyed them by tyranny no more cruel deed would ever have been heard of. Nevertheless, he was the cause of their death, for they were killed for his sake. What is the difference, then, between such a raging tyrant and a dangerous war as far as the many good and innocent people who perish in it are concerned? Indeed, a wicked tyrant is more tolerable than a bad war, as you must admit from your own reason and experience.

I can easily believe that you would like to have peace and good times, but suppose God prevents this by war or tyrants! Now, make up your mind whether you would rather have war or tyrants, for you are guilty enough to have deserved both from God. However, we are the kind of people who want to be scoundrels and live in sin and yet we want to avoid the punishment of sin, and even resist punishment and defend our skin. We shall have about as much success at that as a dog has when he tries to bite through steel.

In the third place, if the rulers are wicked, what of it? God is still around, and he has fire, water, iron, stone, and countless ways of killing. How quickly he can kill a tyrant! He would do it, too, but our sins do not permit it, for he says in Job [34:30], "He permits a knave to rule because of the people's sins." We have no trouble seeing that a scoundrel is ruling. However, no one wants to see that he is ruling not because he is a scoundrel, but because of the people's sin. The people do not look at their own sin; they think that the tyrant rules because he is such a scoundrel—that is how blind, perverse, and mad the world is! That is why things happened the way they did when the peasants revolted. They wanted to punish the sins of the rulers, as though they themselves were pure and guiltless; therefore God had to show them the log in their eye so they would forget about the speck in another man's eye [Matt. 7:3-5].

In the fourth place, the tyrants run the risk that, by God's decree, their subjects may rise up, as has been said, and kill them or expel them. For here we are giving instruction to those who want to do what is right, and they are very few. The great multitude remain heathen, godless, and un-Christian; and these, if God so decrees, wrongfully rise up against the rulers and create disaster, as the Jews and Greeks and Romans often did. Therefore you have no right to complain that our doctrine gives the tyrants and rulers security to do evil; on the contrary, they are certainly not secure. We teach, to be sure, that they ought to be secure, whether they do good or evil. However, we can neither give them this security nor guarantee it for them, for we cannot compel the multitude to follow our teaching if God does not give us grace. We teach what we will, and the world does what it wills. God must help, and we must teach those who are willing to do what is good and right so that they may help hold the multitude in check. The lords are just as secure because of our teaching as they would be without it. Unfortunately, your complaint is unnecessary, since most of the crowd does not listen to us. The preservation of the rulers whom God has appointed is a matter that rests with God and in his hands alone. We experienced this in the peasants' rebellion. Therefore do not be misled by the wickedness of the rulers; their punishment and disaster are nearer than you might wish. Dionysius, the tyrant of Syracuse, confessed that his life was like the life of a man over whose head a sword hung by a silken thread and under whom a glowing fire was burning.

In the fifth place, God has still another way to punish rulers, so that there is no need for you to avenge yourselves. He can raise up foreign rulers, as he raised up the Goths against the Romans, the Assyrians against the Jews, etc. Thus there is vengeance, punishment, and danger enough hanging over tyrants and rulers, and God does not allow them to be wicked and have peace and joy. He is right behind them; indeed, he surrounds them and has them between spurs and under bridle. This also agrees with the natural law that Christ teaches in Matthew 7 [:12], "Whatever you wish that men would do to you, do so to them." Obviously, no father would want his own family to drive him out of the house, kill him, or ruin him because he had done things that were wrong, especially if his family did it maliciously and used force to avenge themselves without previously having brought charges against him before a higher authority. It ought to be just as wrong for any subject to treat his tyrant in such a way.

* * *

"But," you say, "suppose that a king or lord has given an oath to his subjects to rule according to articles that have been agreed upon and then does not keep the agreement.   He thereby forfeits his right to rule. It is said that the king of France must rule according to the parlements, and that the king of Denmark must also swear to certain articles, etc."   Here is my answer: It is right and proper for rulers to govern according to laws and administer them and not to rule arbitrarily. I add, however, that a king does not only promise to keep the law of his land or the articles of election, but God himself commands him to be righteous, and he promises to do so. Well, then, if this king keeps neither God's law nor the law of the land, ought you to attack him, judge him, and take vengeance on him? Who commanded you to do that? Another ruler would have to come between you, hear both sides, and condemn the guilty party; otherwise you will not escape the judgment of God, who says, "Vengeance is mine" [Rom. 12:19], and again, "Judge not" (Matthew 7 [:1]).

* * *

Moreover, I do not want anyone to think that what I have written here applies only to peasants, as though they were the only ones of lower rank and the nobles were not also subjects. Not at all! What I say about "subjects" is intended for peasants, citizens of the cities, nobles, counts, and princes as well. For all of these have overlords and are the subjects of someone else. A rebellious noble, count, or prince should have his head cut off the same as a rebellious peasant. The one should be treated like the other, and no one will be treated unjustly.

I believe Emperor Maximilian could have sung a pretty little song about rebellious princes and nobles who put their heads together to start a rebellion. And the nobles! How often have they complained and conspired and sought to defy the princes and rebel? Think of the furor the Franconian nobles alone have made about how little they care for the emperor or for their bishops. However, we are not supposed to call these knightlets   rebels or troublemakers, although that is exactly what they were. The peasant, on the other hand, is supposed to stand for it and keep quiet. But unless my mind deceives me, God has punished the rebellious lords and nobles through the rebellious peasants, one scoundrel with another. Maximilian had to put up with these nobles and could not punish them, though he had to restrain the peasants as long as he lived. The situation in Germany was so critical that I would be willing to wager that if the peasants had not revolted, a rebellion would have broken out among the nobles against the princes and perhaps against the emperor. But now the peasants are the ones who have revolted and they alone have become the villains. As a result the nobles and the princes get off easy and can wipe their mouths as though they had done nothing wrong. But God is not deceived [Gal. 6:7]; he has used these events to warn the nobles that they, too, should learn to obey their rulers. Let this be my flattery of princes and lords!

Here you say, "Are we, then, to put up with a ruler who would be such a scoundrel that he lets land and people go to ruin?" To say it as the nobles would, "Devil! St. Vitus' Dance! Pestilence! St. Anthony! St. Quirinus! * I am a nobleman and am I supposed to allow my wife and children and body and property to be so shamefully ruined?" I reply: Listen here! I am not trying to teach you anything. Go ahead and do what you please! You are smart enough. You do not need me! I do not have to worry about anything except watching while you sing this proud little song to the bitter end.

To the others, who would like to keep their conscience clear, we have this to say: God has thrown us into the world, under the power of the devil. As a result, we have no paradise here. Rather, at any time we can expect all kinds of misfortune to body, wife, child, property, and honor. And if there is one hour in which there are less than ten disasters or an hour in which we can even survive, we ought to say, "How good God is to me! He has not sent every disaster to me in this one hour." How is that possible? Indeed, as long as I live under the devil's power, I should not have one happy hour. That is what we teach our people. Of course, you may do something else. You may build yourself a paradise where the devil cannot get in so that you need not expect the rage of any tyrant. We will watch you! Actually things go too well for us. We are too happy and content. We do not know how good

God is to us and we believe neither that God takes care of us nor that the devil is so evil. We want to be nothing but wicked scoundrels and yet receive nothing but good from God.

That is enough on the first point, that is, that war and uprisings against our superiors cannot be right. However, people do and are in danger of doing this every day, just as they do everything else that is evil and unjust. But when it comes from God and he does not prevent it, the final outcome is not good and the people involved suffer, even though such rebels seem to have good fortune for a while.

Now we will move on to the second point and discuss the question whether equals may wage war against equals. I would have this understood as follows: It is not right to start a war just because some silly lord has gotten the idea into his head. At the very outset I want to say that whoever starts a war is in the wrong. And it is only right and proper that he who first draws his sword is defeated, or even punished, in the end. This is what has usually happened in history. Those who have started wars have lost them, and those who fought in self-defense have only seldom been defeated. Worldly government has not been instituted by God to break the peace and start war, but to maintain peace and to avoid war. Paul says in Romans 13 [:4] that it is the duty of the sword to protect and punish, to protect the good in peace and to punish the wicked with war. God tolerates no injustice and he has so ordered things that warmongers must be defeated in war. As the proverb says, "No one has ever been so evil that he does not meet someone more evil than he is." And in Psalm 68 [:30] God has the psalmist sing of him, *"Dissipat gentes, quae bella volunt,"* that is, "He scatters the peoples who delight in war."

Beware, therefore; God does not lie! Take my advice. Make the broadest possible distinction between what you want to do and what you ought to do, between desire and necessity, between lust for war and willingness to fight.

* * *

Let this be, then, the first thing to be said in this matter: No war is just, even if it is a war between equals, unless one has such a good reason for fighting and such a good conscience that he can say, "My neighbor compels and forces me to fight, though I would rather avoid it." In that case, it can be called not only war, but lawful self-defense, for we must distinguish between wars that someone begins because that is what he wants to do and does before anyone else attacks him, and those wars that are provoked when an attack is made by someone else. The first kind can be called wars of desire; the second, wars of necessity.

* * *

This is the first thing to be said in this matter. The second should be just as carefully observed. Even though you are absolutely certain that you are not starting a war but are being forced into one, you should still fear God and remember him. You should not march out to war saying, "Ah, now I have been forced to fight and have good cause for going to war." You ought not to think that that justifies anything you do and plunge headlong into battle. It is indeed true that you have a really good reason to go to war and to defend yourself, but that does not give you God's guarantee that you will win. Indeed, such confidence may result in your defeat—even though you have a just cause for fighting the war— for God cannot endure such pride and confidence except in a man who humbles himself before him and fears him. He is pleased with the man who fears neither man nor devil and is bold and confident, brave and firm against both, if they began the war and are in the wrong. But there is nothing to the idea that this will produce a victory, as though it were our deeds or power that did it. Rather, God wants to be feared . . .

* * *

Our conclusion on this point, then, is that war against equals should be waged only when it is forced upon us and then it should be fought in the fear of God. Such a war is forced upon us when an enemy or neighbor attacks and starts the war, and refuses to co-operate in settling the matter according to law or through arbitration and common agreement, or when one overlooks and puts up with the enemy's evil words and tricks, but he still insists on having his own way. I am assuming throughout that I am preaching to those who want to do what is right in God's sight. Those who will neither offer nor consent to do what is right do not concern me. Fearing God means that we do not rely on the justness of our cause, but that we are careful, diligent, and cautious, even in the very smallest details, in so small a thing as a whistle. With all this, however, God's hands are not bound so that he cannot bid us make war against those who have not given us just cause, as he did when he commanded the children of Israel to go to war against the Canaanites. In such a case God's command is necessity enough. However, even such a war should not be fought without fear and care, as God shows in Joshua 3 [7:1-5] when the children of Israel marched confidently against the men of Ai, and were beaten. The same kind of necessity arises if subjects fight at the command of their rulers; for God commands us to obey our rulers [Rom. 13:1], and his command requires that we fight, though this too must be done with fear and humility. We shall discuss this further below.

The third question is whether overlords have the right to go to war with their subjects. We have, indeed, heard above that subjects are to be obedient and are even to suffer wrong from their tyrants. Thus, if things go well, the rulers have nothing to do with their subjects except to cultivate fairness, righteousness, and judgment. However, if the subjects rise up and rebel, as the peasants did recently, then it is right and proper to fight against them. That, too, is what a prince should do to his nobles and an emperor to his princes if they are rebellious and start a war. Only it must be done in the fear of God, and too much reliance must not be placed on being in the right, lest God determine that the lords are to be punished by their subjects, even though the subjects are in the wrong. This has often happened, as we have heard above. For to be right and to do right do not always go together. Indeed, they never go together unless God joins them. Therefore, although it is right that subjects patiently suffer everything and do not revolt, nevertheless, it is not for men to decide whether they shall do so. For God has appointed subjects to care for themselves as individuals, has taken the sword from them, and has put it into the hands of another. If they rebel against this, get others to join them and break loose, and take the sword, then before God they are worthy of condemnation and death.

Overlords, on the other hand, are appointed to be persons who exist for the sake of the community,   and not for themselves alone. They are to have the support of their subjects and are to bear the sword. Compared to his overlord the emperor, a prince is not a prince, but an individual who owes obedience to the emperor, as do all others, each for himself. But when he is seen in relationship to his own subjects he is as many persons as he has people under him and attached to him. So the emperor, too, when compared with

God, is not an emperor, but an individual person like all others; compared with his subjects, however, he is as many times emperor as he has people under him. The same thing can be said of all other rulers. When compared to their overlord, they are not rulers at all and are stripped of all authority. When compared with their subjects, they are adorned with all authority.

Thus, in the end, all authority comes from God, whose alone it is; for he is emperor, prince, count, noble, judge, and all else, and he assigns these offices to his subjects as he wills, and takes them back again for himself. Now no individual ought to set himself against the community or attract the support of the community to himself, for in so doing he is chopping over his head, and the chips will surely fall in his eyes.   From this you see that those who resist their rulers resist the ordinance of God, as St. Paul teaches in Romans 13 [:2]. In I Corinthians 15 [:24] Paul also says that God will abolish all authority when he himself shall reign and return all things to himself.

So much on these three points; now come the questions. Now since no king can go to war alone (any more than he can administer the law courts alone—he must have people who serve him in war just as he must have counselors, judges, lawyers, jailers, executioners, and whatever else is necessary for the administration of justice), the question arises whether a man ought to hire himself out for wages, *dienstgelt* or *mangelt* as they call it, and commit himself to serve the prince as the occasion may demand, as is customary.

* * *

In Luke 2 [3:14] St. John the Baptist confirms the right of this first class to their pay and to hold fiefs, and says that they rightly do their duty when they help their lord make war and serve him. When the soldiers asked him what they were to do, he answered, "Be content with your wages." Now if it were wrong for them to take wages, or if their occupation were against God, he could not have let it continue, permitted it, and confirmed it, but, as a godly, Christian teacher, he would have had to condemn it and deter them from it. This is the answer to those who, because of tenderness of conscience—though this is now rare among these people—profess that it is dangerous to take up this occupation for the sake of temporal goods, since it is nothing but bloodshed, murder, and the inflicting of all kinds of suffering upon one's neighbor, as happens in wartime.

These men should inform their consciences that they do not do this from choice, desire, or ill-will, but that this is God's work and that it is their duty to their prince and their God. Therefore, since it is a legitimate office, ordained by God, they should be paid and compensated for doing it, as Christ says in Matthew 10 [:10], "A laborer deserves his wage."

Of course, it is true that if a man serves as a soldier with a heart that neither seeks nor thinks of anything but acquiring wealth, and if temporal wealth is his only reason for doing it, he is not happy when there is peace and not war. Such a man strays from the path and belongs to the devil, even though he fights out of obedience to his lord and at his call. He takes a work that is good in itself and makes it bad for himself by not being very concerned about serving out of obedience and duty, but only about seeking his own profit.

* * *

A second question: "Suppose my lord were wrong in going to war." I reply: If you know for sure that he is wrong, then you should fear God rather than men, Acts 4 [5:29], and you should neither fight nor serve, for you cannot have a good conscience before God. "Oh, no," you say, "my lord would force me to do it; he would take away my fief and would not give me my money, pay, and wages. Besides, I would be despised and put to shame as a coward, even worse, as a man who did not keep his word and deserted his lord in need." I answer: You must take that risk and, with God's help, let whatever happens, happen. He can restore it to you a hundredfold, as he promises in the gospel, "Whoever leaves house, farm, wife, and property, will receive a hundredfold," etc. [Matt. 19:29].

In every other occupation we are also exposed to the danger that the rulers will compel us to act wrongly; but since God will have us leave even father and mother for his sake, we must certainly leave lords for his sake. But if you do not know, or cannot find out, whether your lord is wrong, you ought not to weaken certain obedience for the sake of an uncertain justice; rather you should think the best of your lord, as is the way of love, for "love believes all things" and "does not think evil," I Corinthians 13 [:4-7]. So, then, you are secure and walk well before God. If they put you to shame or call you disloyal, it is better for God to call you loyal and honorable than for the world to call you loyal and honorable.

What good would it do you if the world thought of you as a Solomon or a Moses, and in God's judgment you were considered as bad as Saul or Ahab?

The third question: "Can a soldier obligate himself to serve more than one lord and take wages or salary from each?" Answer: I said above that greed is wrong, whether in a good or an evil occupation. Agriculture is certainly one of the best occupations; nonetheless, a greedy farmer is wrong and is condemned before God. So in this case to take wages is just and right, and to serve for wages is also right. But greed is not right, even though the wages for the whole year were less than a gulden. Again, to take wages and serve for them is right in itself; it does not matter whether the wages come from one, or two, or three, or however many lords, so long as your hereditary lord or prince is not deprived of what is due him and your service to others is rendered with his will and consent. A craftsman may sell his skill to anyone who will have it, and thus serve the one to whom he sells it, so long as this is not against his ruler and his community. In the same way a soldier has his skill in fighting from God and can use it in the service of whoever desires to have it, exactly as though his skill were an art or trade, and he can take pay for it as he would for his work. For the soldier's vocation also springs from the law of love. If anyone needs me and calls for me, I am at his service, and for this I take my wage or whatever is given me. This is what St. Paul says in I Corinthians 9 [:7], "Who serves as a soldier at his own expense?" Thereby Paul approves the soldier's right to his salary. If a prince needs and requires another's subject for fighting, the subject, with his own prince's consent and knowledge, may serve and take pay for it.

* * *

The fourth question: "What is to be said about the man who goes to war not only for the sake of wealth, but also for the sake of temporal honor, to become a big man and be looked up to?" Answer: Greed for money and greed for honor are both greed; the one is as wrong as the other. Whoever goes to war because of this vice earns hell for himself. We should leave and give all honor to God alone and be satisfied with our wages and rations.

It is, therefore, a heathen and not a Christian custom to exhort soldiers before the battle with words like this, "Dear comrades, dear soldiers, be brave and confident; God willing, we shall this day win honor and become rich." On the contrary, they should be exhorted like this, "Dear comrades, we are gathered here to serve, obey, and do our duty to our prince, for according to God's will and ordinance we are bound to support our prince with our body and our possessions, even though in God's sight we are as poor sinners as our enemies are. Nevertheless, since we know that our prince is in the right in this case, or at least do not know otherwise, we are therefore sure and certain that in serving and obeying him we are serving God. Let everyone, then, be brave and courageous and let no one think otherwise than that his fist is God's fist, his spear God's spear, and cry with heart and voice, 'For God and the emperor!' If God gives us victory, the honor and praise shall be his, not ours, for he wins it through us poor sinners. But we will take the booty and the wages as presents and gifts of God's goodness and grace to us, though we are unworthy, and sincerely thank him for them. Now God grant the victory! Forward with joy!"

ON WAR
AGAINST THE TURK

1529

Translated by Charles M. Jacobs

Revised by Robert C. Schultz

With the defeat of King Louis II of Hungary in 1526 the European fear of the Turks had intensified. Internal problems within the Ottoman Empire had kept the Turks from capitalizing on this victory, but by 1528 they were again threatening. There was great confusion as to the best response. Some called for pacifism as the only Christian response; others argued that the Turks were relatively benign rulers and capitulation was the best solution; still others called for a holy crusade against the infidels. Many friends had pressed Luther to sort out the problem and provide guidance for the Christian. Luther published the tract in April, 1529. The text below is from *LW* 46, 161–205 passim.

Pope Leo X in the bull in which he put me under the ban condemned, among other statements, the following one, "To fight against the Turk is the same as resisting God, who visits our sin upon us with this rod." This may be why they say that I oppose and dissuade from war against the Turk. I do not hesitate to admit that this article is mine and that I stated and defended it at the time; and if things in the world were in the same state now that they were in then, I would still have to hold and defend it. But it is not fair to forget what the situation was then and what my grounds and reasons were, and to take my words and apply them to another situation where those grounds and reasons do not exist. With this kind of skill who could not make the gospel a pack of lies or pretend that it contradicted itself?

This was the state of things at that time: no one had taught, no one had heard, and no one knew anything about temporal government, whence it came, what its office and work were, or how it ought to serve God. The most learned men (I shall not name them) regarded temporal government as a heathen, human, ungodly thing, as though it jeopardized salvation to be in the ranks of the rulers. This is how the priests and monks drove kings and princes into the corner and persuaded them that to serve God they must undertake other works, such as hearing mass, saying prayers, endowing masses,* etc. In a word, princes and lords who wanted to be pious men regarded their rank and office as of no value and did not consider it a service of God. They became real priests and monks, except that they did not wear tonsures and cowls. If they wanted to serve God, they had to go to church. All the lords living at that time would have to testify to this, for they knew it by experience. My gracious lord, Duke Frederick, of blessed memory, was so glad when I first wrote *Temporal Authority* that he had the little book copied and put in a special binding, and was happy that he could see what his position was in God's sight.

And so it was that at that time the pope and the clergy were all in all and through all, like God in the world [Eph. 4:6], and the temporal rulers were in darkness, oppressed and unknown. But the pope and his crowd wanted to be Christians, too, and therefore they pretended to make war on the Turk. It was over those two points that the discussion arose, for I was then working on doctrine that concerned Christians and the conscience, and had as yet written nothing about temporal rulers. The papists called me a flatterer of princes because I was dealing only with the spiritual class, and not with the temporal; just as they call me seditious now that I have written in such glorification of temporal government as no teacher has done since the days of the apostles, except, perhaps, St. Augustine. I can boast of this with a good conscience, and the testimony of the world will support me.

Among the points of Christian doctrine, I discussed what Christ says in Matthew [5:39-41], namely, that a Christian shall not resist evil, but endure all things, let the coat go and the cloak, let them be taken from him, turn the other cheek, etc. The pope with his universities and cloister schools had made a counsel of this, something which was not commanded and which a Christian need not keep; thus they perverted Christ's word, taught false doctrine throughout the world, and deceived Christians. But since they wanted to be Christians—indeed, the best Christians in the world—and yet fight against the Turk, endure no evil, and suffer neither compulsion nor wrong, I opposed them with these words of Christ that Christians shall not resist evil, but suffer all things and surrender all things. I based the article condemned by Pope Leo upon this. He was eager to condemn it because I took away the cloak covering the Roman knavery.

The popes had never seriously intended to wage war against the Turk; instead they used the Turkish war as a cover for their game and robbed Germany of money by means of indulgences whenever they took the notion. The whole world knew it, but now it is forgotten. So they condemned my article not because it opposed the Turkish war, but because it tore away this cloak and blocked the path along which the money went to Rome. If they had seriously wished to fight the Turk, the pope and the cardinals would have had enough from the pallia, annates,* and other unmentionable sources of income so that they would not have needed to practice such extortion and robbery in Germany. If there had been a general opinion that a serious war was at hand, I could have polished my article somewhat more and made some distinctions.

Nor did I like it that the Christians and the princes were driven, urged, and irritated into attacking the Turk, and making war on him, before they amended their own ways and lived as true Christians. These two points, or either one by itself, were enough reason to dissuade from war. I shall never advise a heathen or a Turk, let alone a Christian, to attack another or begin war. That is nothing else than advising bloodshed and destruction, and it brings no good fortune in the end, as I have written in the book *Whether Soldiers, Too, Can Be Saved*; and it never does any good when one rascal punishes another without first becoming good himself.

But what motivated me most of all was this: They undertook to fight against the Turk in the name of Christ, and taught and incited men to do this, as though our people were an army of Christians against the Turks, who were enemies of Christ. This is absolutely contrary to Christ's doctrine and name. It is against his doctrine because he says that Christians shall not resist evil, fight, or quarrel, nor take revenge or insist on rights [Matt. 5:39]. It is against his name because there are scarcely five Christians in such an army, and perhaps there are worse people in the eyes of God in that army than are the Turks; and yet they all want to bear the name of Christ. This is the greatest of all sins and is one that no Turk commits, for Christ's name is used for sin and shame and thus dishonored. This would be especially so if the pope and the bishops were involved in the war, for they would bring the greatest shame and dishonor to Christ's name because they are called to fight against the devil with the word of God and with prayer, and they would be deserting their calling and office to fight with the sword against flesh and blood. They are not commanded to do this; it is forbidden.

O how gladly Christ would receive me at the Last Judgment if, when summoned to the spiritual office to preach and care for souls, I had left it and busied myself with fighting and with the temporal sword! Why should Christ or his people have anything to do with the sword and going to war, and kill men's bodies, when he declared that he has come to save the world, not to kill people [John 3:17]? His work is to deal with the gospel and to redeem men from sin and death by his Spirit to help them from this world to everlasting life. According to John 6 [:15] he fled and would not let himself be made king; before Pilate he confessed, "My kingship is not of this world" [John 18:36]; and in the garden he bade Peter to put up his sword and said, "All who take the sword will perish by the sword" [Matt. 26:52].

I say this not because I would teach that worldly rulers ought not be Christians, or that a Christian cannot bear the sword and serve God in temporal government. Would to God they were all Christians, or that no one could be a prince unless he were a Christian! Things would be better than they now are, and the Turk would not be so powerful. But what I want to do is to keep a distinction between the callings and offices, so that everyone can see to what God has called him and fulfil the duties of his office faithfully and sincerely in the service of God. I have written more than enough about this elsewhere, especially in the books *Whether Soldiers, Too, Can Be Saved* and *Temporal Authority*. In the church, where all should be Christians, Paul will not permit one person to assume another's office, Romans 12 [:4] and I Corinthians 12 [:14-26], but exhorts every member to do his own work so that there be no disorder, rather, that everything be done in an orderly way [I Cor. 14:40]. How much less, then, are we to tolerate the disorder that arises when a Christian abandons his office and assumes a temporal office, or when a bishop or pastor gives up his office and assumes the office of a prince or judge; or, on the other hand, when a prince takes up the office of a bishop and gives up his princely office? Even today this shameful disorder rages and rules in the whole papacy, contrary to their own canons and laws.

* * *

It is true, indeed, that since they have temporal lordship and wealth, they ought to make the same contributions to the emperor, kings, or princes that other possessors of holdings properly make, and render the same services that others are expected to render. Indeed, these "goods of the church," as they call them, ought to be used especially and first of all to serve and help in the protection of the needy and the welfare of all classes, for that is the purpose for which they were given, not for a bishop to give up his office and use these goods for war or battle. If the banner of Emperor Charles or of a prince is in the field, then let everyone run boldly and gladly to the banner to which his allegiance is sworn—more on this will be said later. But if the banner of a bishop, cardinal, or pope is there, then run the other way, and say, "I do not know this coin;   if it were a prayer book, or the Holy Scriptures preached in the church, I would rally to it."

Now before I exhort or urge war against the Turk, hear me, for God's sake. I want first to teach you how to fight with a good conscience. For although (if I wanted to give way to the old Adam) I could keep quiet and look on while the Turk avenged me upon the tyrants (who persecute the gospel and blame me for all kinds of misfortune) and paid them back for it, nevertheless, I shall not do this, but rather, shall serve both friends and enemies so that my sun may rise on both bad and good, and my rain fall on the thankful and unthankful [Matt. 5:45].

In the first place, the Turk certainly has no right or command to begin war and to attack lands that are not his. Therefore his war is nothing but an outrage and robbery with which God is punishing the world, as he often does through wicked scoundrels, and sometimes through godly people. The Turk does not fight from necessity or to protect his land in peace, as the right kind of a ruler does; but, like a pirate or highwayman, he seeks to rob and ravage other lands which do and have done nothing to him. He is God's rod and the devil's servant [Isa. 10:5]; there is no doubt about that.

In the second place, we must know who the man is who is to

make war against the Turk so that he may be certain that he has a commission from God and is doing right. He must not plunge in to avenge himself or have some other mad notion or reason. He must be sure of this so that, win or lose, he may be in a state of salvation and in a godly occupation. There are two of these men, and there ought to be only two: the one is named Christian, the other, Emperor Charles.

Christian should be there first, with his army. Since the Turk is the rod of the wrath of the Lord our God and the servant of the raging devil, the first thing to be done is to smite the devil, his lord, and take the rod out of God's hand, so that the Turk may be found only, in his own strength, all by himself, without the devil's help and without God's hand. This should be done by Sir Christian, that is, by the pious, holy, precious body of Christians. They are the people who have the arms for this war and they know how to use them. If the Turk's god, the devil, is not beaten first, there is reason to fear that the Turk will not be so easy to beat. Now the devil is a spirit who cannot be beaten with armor, muskets, ... Christian weapons and power must do it.

Here you ask, "Who are the Christians and where does one find them?" Answer: There are not many of them, but they are everywhere, though they are spread thin and live far apart, under good and bad princes. Christendom must continue to the end, as the article of the creed says, "I believe one holy Christian church." So it must be possible to find them. Every pastor and preacher ought diligently to exhort his people to repentance and to prayer. They ought to drive men to repentance by showing our great and numberless sins and our ingratitude, by which we have earned God's wrath and disfavor, so that he justly gives us into the hands of the devil and the Turk. And so that this preaching may work the more strongly, they ought to cite examples and sayings from the Scriptures, such as the Flood [Gen. 7:1-24], Sodom and Gomorrah [Gen. 19:24-28], and the children of Israel, and show how cruelly and how often God punished the world and its lands and peoples. And they ought to make it plain that it is no wonder, since we sin more grievously than they did, if we are punished worse than they.

This fight must be begun with repentance, and we must reform our lives, or we shall fight in vain . . .

* * *

After people have thus been taught and exhorted to confess their sin and amend their ways they should then be most diligently exhorted to prayer and shown that such prayer pleases God, that he has commanded it and promised to hear it, and that no one ought to think lightly of his own praying or have doubts about it, but with firm faith be sure that it will be heard; all of which has been published by us in many tracts. The man who doubts, or prays for good luck, would do better to let prayer alone because such prayer is merely tempting God and only makes things worse. Therefore I would advise against processions, which are a heathenish and useless practice, for they are more pomp and show than prayer. I say the same thing about celebrating a lot of masses and calling upon the saints. It might, indeed, be of some use to have the people, especially the young people, sing the Litany at mass or vespers or in the church after the sermon, provided that everyone, even at home by himself, constantly raised to Christ at least a sigh of the heart for grace to lead a better life and for help against the Turk. I am not speaking of much and long praying, but of frequent brief sighs, in one or two words, such as, "O help us, dear God the Father; have mercy on us, dear Lord Jesus Christ!" or the like.

See, now, this kind of preaching will hit home with Christians and find them out, and there will be Christians who will accept it and act according to it; it does not matter if you do not know who they are. The tyrants and bishops may also be exhorted to stop their raging and persecution against the word of God and not to hinder our prayer; but if they do not stop, we must not cease to pray, but keep on and take the chance that they will have the benefit of our prayer and be preserved along with us, or that we shall pay for their raging and be ruined along with them. They are so perverse and blind that if God gave them good fortune against the Turk they would ascribe it to their holiness and merit and boast of it against us. On the other hand, if things turned out bad, they would ascribe it to no one but us, and lay the blame on us, disregarding the shameful, openly sinful, and wicked lives which they not only lead, but defend; for they cannot teach rightly a single point about the way to pray, and they are worse than the Turks. Oh, well, we must leave that to God's judgment.

* * *

The great need of our time should have moved us to this prayer against the Turk, for the Turk, as has been said, is the servant of the devil, who not only devastates land and people with the sword, as we shall hear later, but also lays waste the Christian faith and our dear Lord Jesus Christ. For although some praise the Turk's government because he allows everyone to believe what he will so long as he remains the temporal lord, yet this reputation is not true, for he does not allow Christians to come together in public, and no one can openly confess Christ or preach or teach against Mohammed. What kind of freedom of belief is it when no one is allowed to preach or confess Christ, and yet our salvation depends on that confession, as Paul says in Romans 10 [:9], "To confess with the lips saves," and Christ has strictly commanded us to confess and teach his gospel. *

Since, therefore, faith must be stilled and held in secret among this wild and barbarous people and under this severe rule, how can it exist or remain alive in the long run, when it requires so much effort and labor in places where it is preached most faithfully and diligently? Therefore it happens, and must happen, that those Christians who are captured or otherwise get into Turkey fall away and become altogether Turkish, and it is very seldom that one remains true to his faith, for they lack the living bread of the soul and see the abandoned and carnal life of the Turks and are obliged to adapt themselves to it.

How can one injure Christ more than with these two things, namely, force and wiles? With force they prevent preaching and suppress the word. With wiles they put wicked and dangerous examples before men's eyes every day and draw men to them. So in order not to lose our Lord Jesus Christ, his word and faith, we must pray against the Turks as against other enemies of our salvation and of all good, indeed, as we pray against the devil himself.

* * *

I have wanted to tell all this to the first man, namely, Christian, so that he may know and see how much need there is for prayer, and how he must first smite the Turk's Allah, that is, his god the devil, and overcome his power and divinity; otherwise, I fear, the sword will accomplish little. Now this man is not to fight physically with the Turk, as the pope and his followers teach; nor is he to resist the Turk with the fist, but he is to recognize the Turk as God's rod and wrath which Christians must either suffer, if God visits their sins upon them, or fight against and drive away with repentance, tears, and prayer. Let whoever will despise this counsel despise it; I will watch to see what damage he will do the Turk.

The second man who ought to fight against the Turk is Emperor Charles, or whoever may be emperor; for the Turk is attacking his subjects and his empire, and it is his duty, as a regular ruler appointed by God, to defend his own. I repeat it here: I would not urge or bid anyone to fight against the Turk unless the first method, mentioned above, that men had first repented and been reconciled to God, etc., had been followed. If anyone wants to go to war in another way, let him take his chances. It is not proper for me to say anything more about it other than to point out everyone's duty and to instruct his conscience.

I see clearly that kings and princes are taking such a foolish and careless attitude toward the Turk that I fear they underestimate God and the Turk too greatly, or perhaps they do not know that the Turk is such a mighty lord that no kingdom or land, whatever it is, is strong enough to resist him alone, unless God performs a miracle. Now I cannot expect any miracle * or special grace of God for Germany unless men amend their ways and honor the word of God differently than they have before. But enough has been said about that for those who will listen. Now we want to speak of the emperor.

In the first place, if there is to be war against the Turk, it should be fought at the emperor's command, under his banner, and in his name. Then everyone can be sure in his conscience that he is obeying the ordinance of God, since we know that the emperor is our true overlord and head and that whoever obeys him in such a case obeys God also, whereas he who disobeys him also disobeys God. If he dies in this obedience, he dies in a good state, and if he has previously repented and believes in Christ, he will be saved. I suppose everyone knows these things better than I can teach him, and would to God they knew them as well as they think they do. Yet we will say something more about them.

In the second place, this fighting under the emperor's banner and obedience to him ought to be true and simple. The emperor should seek nothing else than simply to perform the work and duty of his office, which is to protect his subjects; and those under his banner should seek simply to do the work and duty of obedience. By this simplicity you should understand that you are not fighting the Turk for the reasons the emperors and princes have been urged to go to war for, such as the winning of great honor, glory, and wealth, the extension of territory, or wrath and revenge and other such reasons. By waging war for these reasons men seek only their own self-interest, not what is right or to obey, and so we have had no good fortune up to now, either in fighting or planning to fight against the Turk.

Therefore the urging and inciting with which the emperor and the princes have been stirred up to fight against the Turk ought to cease. He has been urged, as head of Christendom and as protector of the church and defender of the faith, to wipe out the Turk's religion, and the urging and exhorting have been based on the wickedness and vice of the Turks. Not so! The emperor is not the head of Christendom or defender of the gospel or the faith. The church and the faith must have a defender other than emperor and kings. They are usually the worst enemies of Christendom and of the faith, as Psalm 2 [:2] says and as the church constantly laments. That kind of urging and exhorting only makes things worse and angers God deeply because it interferes with his honor and his work, and would ascribe it to men, which is idolatry and blasphemy.

And if the emperor were supposed to destroy the unbelievers and non-Christians, he would have to begin with the pope, bishops, and clergy, and perhaps not spare us or himself; for there is enough horrible idolatry in his own empire to make it unnecessary for him to fight the Turks for this reason. There are entirely too many Turks, Jews, heathen, and non-Christians among us with open false doctrine and with offensive, shameful lives. Let the Turk believe and live as he will, just as one lets the papacy and other false Christians live. The emperor's sword has nothing to do with the faith; it belongs to physical, worldly things, if God is not to become angry with us. If we pervert his order and throw it into confusion, he too becomes perverse and throws us into confusion and all kinds of misfortune, as it is written, "With the crooked thou dost show thyself perverse" [Ps. 18:26]. We can perceive and grasp this through the fortune we have had up to now against the Turk. Think of all the heartbreak and misery that have been caused by the *cruciata*,[*] by the indulgences, and by crusade taxes. With these Christians have been stirred up to take the sword and fight the Turk when they ought to have been fighting the devil and unbelief with the word and with prayer.

Here is what should be done. The emperor and the princes should be exhorted concerning their office and their bounden duty to give serious and constant thought to governing their subjects in peace and to protecting them against the Turk. This would be their duty whether they themselves were Christians or not, though it would be very good if they were Christians. But since it is and remains uncertain whether they are Christians, and it is certain that they are emperors and princes, that is, that they have God's command to protect their subjects and are duty bound to do so, we must let the uncertain go and hold to the certain,   urge them with continual preaching and exhortation, and lay it heavily upon their consciences that it is their duty to God not to let their subjects perish so terribly, and that they commit serious sin when they are not mindful of their office and do not use all their power to bring counsel and help to those who should live, with body and goods, under their protection and who are bound to them by oaths of homage.

* * *

I wish it clearly understood, however, that it was not for nothing that I called Emperor Charles the man who ought to go to war against the Turk.   As for other kings, princes, and rulers who despise Emperor Charles, or are not his subjects, or are not obedient, I leave them to take their own chances. They shall do nothing because of my advice or admonition; what I have written here is for Emperor Charles and his subjects; the others do not concern me. I know quite well the pride of some kings and princes who would be glad if it were not Emperor Charles, but they, who were to be the heroes and victors who win honor against the Turk. I grant them the honor, but if they are beaten, it will be their own fault. Why do they not conduct themselves humbly toward the true head and the proper ruler? The rebellion among the peasants was punished, but if the rebellion among the princes and lords were also to be punished, I think that there would be very few princes and lords left.   God grant that it may not be the Turk who inflicts the punishment! Amen.

DR. MARTIN LUTHER'S WARNING
TO HIS DEAR GERMAN PEOPLE

1531

Translated by Martin H. Bertram

After the Diet of Augsburg the Emperor Charles V declared that
the Lutherans had been thoroughly refuted, and he proclaimed
(September, 1530) a six-month period for all princes to remove the
Lutheran heresy from the empire. There existed the imminent possibility that the emperor would use force to wipe out the Reformation. The problem of a justified resistance to the emperor was thus
foremost in the minds of Protestant rulers and subjects. Jurist ad-
visors to the Protestant Elector John of Saxony had argued that
resistance was justified. Relying in part on the jurists, Luther is
compelled to reexamine the Christian's obligation to temporal authority in light of these new circumstances. The text below is from
LW 47, 11–55 passim.

I issued an urgent and sincere admonition publicly to the clerical
members of the Diet of Augsburg in which I implored them not to
let the diet—on which all the world set such great hopes and toward
which it looked with longing—adjourn inconclusively, but rather
work toward the establishment of peace, the cessation of some of
their abominations, and freedom for the gospel. I also strove and
sighed for these things with all my might in my prayers before God,
as did all good Christians. However, since neither our diligent
prayer to God nor our sincere warning to them availed, one can
readily infer what this means: namely, that God considers them to
be hardened and blinded; they are guilty of so much innocent
blood, blasphemy, and shameful, impenitent living, that he does not
consider that they are worthy to receive a single good thought or

emotion or that they will pay any attention to a word of wholesome and peaceful admonition.

* * *

If worst comes to worst, then one of two things will happen: either a war or a rebellion will occur, perhaps both at the same time. For there is indeed danger—we are now speaking as in a dream, as if there were no God—that if they initiate a war, an armed troop will organize and a mob band together, perhaps even among their own people, so that both they and we will perish. For in such an event they cannot rely on our teaching and take it for granted that no one will attack them, just because we wrote and taught so emphatically not to resort to rebellion, but to suffer the madness even of tyrants, and not to defend oneself. This is what I teach, but I cannot create the doers of this teaching, since they esteem so little all the other articles of our teaching. If now the masses should reject our teaching against rebellion, especially if they were provoked by such a godless outrage and wanton war, then the devil would make real fools of them and expose them very nicely and neatly. I am still speaking in a dream. But let them see to it that the dream does not come true. The dream does not harm me, but if it hits them, so be it.

All right, if a war or a rebellion should break out as I fear (for God's wrath will have to take its course), I wish to testify before God and all the world here in this writing that we, who are derisively called "Lutherans," neither counseled it or consented to it, nor, indeed, gave any cause for it; rather we constantly and ceaselessly pleaded and called for peace. The papists themselves know and have to admit that we have preached peace up till now and have also kept the peace, and that peace was also our ardent desire now at the diet. Consequently, if a war or a rebellion should break out, it can under no circumstances be said, "See, that is the fruit of Lutheran teaching." It will rather have to be said, "See, that is the papists' teaching and its fruit; they want peace neither for themselves nor for others." Until now we have taught and lived quietly. We drew no sword and did not burn, murder, or rob anyone, as they have done in the past and still do; rather we endured their murder and pillage, their raving and raging with the greatest patience.

Furthermore, when our people were threatened and challenged, defied, jeered, and mocked at the diet by the papists, they humbled themselves most abjectly and let themselves simply be trampled underfoot. Despite all, they asked and pleaded for peace, and they offered to do all that God might want. That would have been more than enough, even if our party were mere beggars, to say nothing of the fact that they are great princes, lords, and godly and honorable people. Therefore, I believe that there have been but few instances of such a confession and of such humility and of such patience as long as Christendom has existed, and I trust this will not be exceeded before the Last Day. Yet all of this was of no avail.

* * *

... it is not fitting for me, a preacher, vested with the spiritual office, to wage war or to counsel war or incite it, but rather to dissuade from war and to direct to peace, as I have done until now with all diligence. All the world must bear witness to this. However, our enemies do not want to have peace, but war. If war should come now, I will surely hold my pen in check and keep silent and not intervene as I did in the last uprising. I will let matters take their course, even though not a bishop, priest, or monk survives and I myself also perish. For their defiance and boasting are intolerable to God; their impenitent heart is carrying things too far. They were begged, they were admonished, they were implored for peace beyond all reasonable measure. They insist on forcing the issue with flesh and blood; so I, too, will force the issue with them through the Spirit and through God and henceforth set not one or two papists but the entire papacy against me, until the Judge in heaven intervenes with signs. I will not and cannot be afraid of such miserable enemies of God. I disdain their defiance, and I laugh at their wrath. They can do no more than deprive me of a sack of ailing flesh. But they shall soon discover of what I am able to deprive them.

Furthermore, if war breaks out—which God forbid—I will not reprove those who defend themselves against the murderous and bloodthirsty papists, nor let anyone else rebuke them as being seditious, but I will accept their action and let it pass as self-defense. I will direct them in this matter to the law and to the jurists. For in such an instance, when the murderers and bloodhounds wish to wage war and to murder, it is in truth no insurrection to rise against them and defend oneself. Not that I wish to incite or spur anyone on to such self-defense, or to justify it, for that is not my office; much less does it devolve on me to pass judgment or sentence on him. A Christian knows very will what he is to do—namely, to render to God the things that are God's and to Caesar the things that are Caesar's [Matt. 22:21], but not to render to the blood-hounds the things that are not theirs. I want to make a distinction between sedition and other acts and to deprive the bloodhounds of the pretext of boasting that they are warring against rebellious people and that they were justified according to both human and divine law; for so the little kitten is fond of grooming and adorning itself. Likewise, I do not want to leave the conscience of the people burdened by the concern and worry that their self-defense might be rebellious. For such a term would be too evil and too harsh in such a case. It should be given a different name, which I am sure the jurists can find for it.

We must not let everything be considered rebellious which the bloodhounds designate as such. For in that way they want to silence the lips and tie the hands of the entire world, so that no one may either reprove them with preaching or defend himself with his fist, while they keep their mouth open and their hands free. Thus they want to frighten and ensnare all the world with the name "insurrection," and at the same time comfort and reassure themselves. No, dear fellow, we must submit to you a different interpretation and definition of that term. To act contrary to law is not rebellion; otherwise every violation of the law would be rebellion. No, he is an insurrectionist who refuses to submit to government and law, who attacks and fights against them, and attempts to overthrow them with a view to making himself ruler and establishing the law, as Münzer did; that is the true definition of a rebel. *Aliud est invasor, aliud transgressor.* * In accordance with this definition, self-defense against the bloodhounds cannot be rebellious. For the papists are deliberately starting the war; they refuse to keep the peace, they do not let others rest who would like to live in peace. Thus the papists are much closer to the name and the quality which is termed rebellion.

* * *

It is also obvious that they are acting contrary to imperial and to natural law; for in the first place, they hardly gave our side a hearing, and then, when they delivered their tardy, flimsy confutation orally, they simply refused to hand us a copy of it, nor did they give us an opportunity to make reply. To the present day they shun the light like bats. It is, of course, in accord with divine, imperial, and natural law, as the heathen Porcius Festus also held in the controversy between the Jews and St. Paul [Acts 25:16], not to condemn a man without a hearing. Even God did not condemn Adam until he first gave him a chance to reply. We appeared voluntarily at Augsburg and offered humbly and eagerly to render an account. This, however, was maliciously and arbitrarily denied us. Nor did they give us their confutation, no matter how often and how much we pleaded for it. Yet we were condemned by the holy fathers in God and by the Christian princes. O excellent teachers! O fine judges, who force all the world to believe and still dare not to publish what is to be believed! I am expected to believe without knowing what to believe. I am told that I am in error, but I am not shown in what I err!

* * *

Yes, you will say, but even though they did not issue their confutation or allow it to be answered, they did appoint instead a committee composed of several princes and scholars from each side and ordered them to discuss the matter at issue in a friendly manner. Little kitten, clean and groom yourself, we are going to have company! * How stupid and foolish is that poor man Christ, not to notice such cunning. The committee did convene, that is true; but what was discussed? Nothing at all about their confutation or refutation; that remained in the dark. The committee had to help in preserving appearances, so as to provide some pretense for keeping the inane confutation under cover and not making it public. For it was not their confutation that was submitted in the committee meeting, but our confession. Their deliberations with our people revolved about such questions as how much of our confession we were willing to drop and withdraw, or how they interpreted it, or how we could make it harmonize with their views. Their one aim and objective was to enable them to make a fine pretense and to raise the hue and cry: "You see, dear people, listen, all the world, and hear how stubborn and stiff-necked the Lutherans are! In the first place, their confession was disproven with Scripture and with well-founded reasons, and then we engaged in friendly discussions with them. What more can we do? They refuse to yield, whether they are overcome or whether instructed in a friendly manner."

* * *

As the confutation is, so is the committee. The confutation is a dark night owl, reluctant to face the light; the committee is sheer cunning and deception. The boast that they tried friendly measures with us is just as truthful and sincere as their boast that they refuted our confession with Holy Scripture and sound reason—both are sheer lying and deceit. To be sure, they would not like to be treated that way by us. However, at present I do not propose to write about the actions of this diet, nor to attack their confutation (though both shall yet be attended to if God wills), but at present I merely wish to show that the papists do not want to have peace, truth, or tranquillity, but insist on enforcing their will and thus are bringing about either a war or an insurrection, whether we like it or not. Nothing will restrain them. We, however, will have to take the risk and await the outcome, since our offers, pleas, and cries for peace are unheeded and our humility and patience go for nought. Let come what cannot be prevented!

But since I am the "prophet of the Germans" —for this haughty title I will henceforth have to assign to myself, to please and oblige my papists and asses—it is fitting that I, as a faithful teacher, warn my dear Germans against the harm and danger threatening them and impart Christian instruction to them regarding their conduct in the event that the emperor, at the instigation of his devils, the papists, issues a call to arms against the princes and cities on our side. It is not that I worry that His Imperial Majesty will listen to such spiteful people and initiate such an unjust war, but I do not want to neglect my duty. I want to keep my conscience clean and unsullied at all events. I would much rather compose a superfluous and unnecessary admonition and warning and impart needless instruction than to neglect my duty and then find, if things go contrary to my expectations, that I am too late and have no other consolation than the words *non putassem,* I did not intend this. The sages suggest making provision for things even if everything is secure. How much less may we trust any wind and weather, no matter how pleasant it may appear, in these difficult times when the papists' raging provokes God's wrath so terribly! Moreover, in Romans 12 Paul commands those who preside over others to look out for them.

Any German who wants to follow my sincere counsel may do so; and whoever does not want to may disregard it. I am not seeking my own benefit in this, but the welfare and salvation of you Germans.

* * *

This is my sincere advice: If the emperor should issue a call to arms against us on behalf of the pope or because of our teaching, as the papists at present horribly gloat and boast—though I do not yet expect this of the emperor—no one should lend himself to it or obey the emperor in this event. All may rest assured that God has strictly forbidden compliance with such a command of the emperor. Whoever does obey him can be certain that he is disobedient to God and will lose both body and soul eternally in the war. For in this case the emperor would not only act in contravention of God and divine law but also in violation of his own imperial law, vow, duty, seal, and edicts. And lest you imagine that this is just my own idea or that such advice is dictated by my fancy, I shall submit clear and strong reasons and arguments to convince you that this is not my own counsel, but God's earnest, manifold, and stringent command. Before his anger you surely ought to be terrified and, in the end, must be terrified.

In the first place, I must say a word in defense of dear Emperor Charles' person. For he has to date, also at the diet, conducted himself in such a way that he has gained the favor and affection of all the world and is worthy of being spared all grief. Our people, too, have nothing but praise for his imperial virtues. Let me cite just a few examples to demonstrate this. It demonstrates a wonderful and rare gentleness of character that His Imperial Majesty refused to condemn our doctrine even though he was vehemently incited and urged on by both the spiritual and secular princes, with unrelenting insistence, even before he left Spain. However, His Majesty stood his ground as firmly as a rock. He hurried to the diet and issued a gracious invitation, wanting to discuss matters in a kind and friendly spirit. He is also reported to have declared: "This cannot be such an utterly evil doctrine, since so many great, exalted, learned, and honest people accept it."

* * *

Furthermore, when the elector of Brandenburg in the recess argued with fine and high-sounding and haughty words that His

Imperial Majesty, the princes, and the estates of the empire had leagued together and were staking land and people, life and property and blood on this, he wanted to intimidate our people with these words. But he failed to add "if God wills," so his words remained mere words and died as soon as they were spoken. When the sound had faded away, no one was afraid. Here His Imperial Majesty again interposed a word. To be sure, he did not say that the speaker was lying, but that he had made an overstatement. Many other great princes and lords were nonplussed and were at a loss to know how to interpret these words. Several suggested that they meant that if our side would attack any of their members by force, then they would ally themselves and come to the defense with life and goods, with blood, land, and people. However, our people never thought of doing that, but always asked and pleaded for peace, as all know very well. Several declared openly before the emperor that they did not concur in this speech of the margrave and that it did not at all reflect their opinion.

It is easy to talk about land and people; but it is another question if anyone has such power over them that he can wager blood, life, and property needlessly and against God and his law. Experience should be able to answer this question. It seems to me that the people will, at least, first have to be consulted, and that one cannot embark on such a venture without announcing it. It should also be remembered that God must not always grant and do what we may venture to think and say. I am sure that the mouths of greater lords have been found to lie miserably and that their schemes thoroughly put them to shame. But the best part of this is that they fail to invoke God in this and that they fail to bear him in mind when they brag so defiantly. However, one can sense the emperor's sentiments in this matter. He is not such a mad bloodhound, and these defiant words do not please him.

* * *

Let this suffice for the time being as an apology for the emperor. Now we want to issue a warning, giving reasons why everyone should rightly beware and fear to obey the emperor in such an instance and to wage war against our side. I repeat what I said earlier, that I do not wish to advise or incite anyone to engage in war. My ardent wish and plea is that peace be preserved and that neither side start a war or give cause for it. For I do not want my conscience burdened, nor do I want to be known before God or the world as having counseled or desired anyone to wage war or to offer resistance except those who are enjoined and authorized to do so (Romans 13). But wherever the devil has so completely possessed the papists that they cannot and will not keep or tolerate peace, or where they absolutely want to wage war or provoke it, that will rest upon their conscience. There is nothing I can do about it, since my remonstrances are ignored and futile.

The first reason why you must not obey the emperor and make war in such an instance as this is that you, as well as the emperor, vowed in baptism to preserve the gospel of Christ and not to persecute it or oppose it. Now you are, of course, aware that in this case the emperor is being incited and duped by the pope to fight against the gospel of Christ, because our doctrine was publicly proved at Augsburg to be the true gospel and Holy Scripture. Therefore, this must be your reply to the emperor's or your prince's summons to arms: "Indeed, dear Emperor, dear prince, if you keep your oath and pledge made in baptism, you will be my dear lord, and I will obey you and go to war at your command. But if you will not keep your baptismal pledge and Christian covenant made with Christ, but rather deny them, then may a rascal obey you in my place. I refuse to blaspheme my God and deny his word for your sake; nor will I impudently rush to spring into the abyss of hell with you."

This first reason has awesome, far-reaching implications. For he who fights and contends against the gospel necessarily fights simultaneously against God, against Jesus Christ, against the Holy Spirit, against the precious blood of Christ, against his death, against God's word, against all the articles of faith, against all the sacraments, against all the doctrines which are given, confirmed, and preserved by the gospel, for example, the doctrine regarding government, regarding worldly peace, worldly estates, in brief, against all angels and saints, against heaven and earth and all creatures. For he who fights against God must fight against all that is of God or that has to do with God. But you would soon discover what kind of end that would lead to! What is even worse, such fighting would be done consciously; for these people know and admit that this teaching is the gospel. The Turks and the Tartars, of course, do not know that it is God's word. Therefore no Turk can be as vile as you, and you must be damned to hell ten times more deeply than all Turks, Tartars, heathen, and Jews.

* * *

The second reason is this: Even if our doctrine were false—although everyone knows it is not—you should still be deterred from fighting solely by the knowledge that by such fighting you are taking upon yourself a part of the guilt before God of all the abominations which have been committed and will yet be committed by the whole papacy. This reason encompasses innumerable loathsome deeds and every vice, sin, and harm. In brief, the bottomless hell itself is found here, with every sin, all of which you share in if you obey the emperor in this instance. We shall enumerate a few of these and bring them into view, lest they be too easily forgotten. For the papists would like to cover themselves and hide such abominations, unrepented and unreformed, until such a time as they can bring them into the open again and restore them.

Here you will first have to take upon yourself the whole of the shameful life which they have led and still lead. They do not intend to mend this; however, you are to shed your blood and risk your life for the protection and preservation of their accursed, shameless life. Then all the whoring, adultery, and fornication rampant in the cathedrals and convents will be on your neck and on your conscience. Your heart will have the honor and glory of having fought for the greatest and most numerous whoremongers and knaves to be found on the earth and for endorsing their 'life of whoring and knavery. You will make yourself a partaker of all of that. Oh, that will be a great honor and a fine reason for risking your life and for serving God. For they will not reform such a life, nor can they reform it, since it is impossible that so many thousands of people should live a chaste life in the way that they try to do it.

Over and above that, you must also burden yourself with the chastity of popes and cardinals. This is a special kind of chastity, transcending the common, spiritual type. In Italian it is termed *buseron,* which is the chastity of Sodom and Gomorrah.

* * *

Furthermore, you will have to encumber yourself with all the greed, robbery, and thievery of the entire papacy, the countless sums they have acquired falsely and fraudulently by means of indulgences. Is it not sheer shameful robbery and thievery throughout all Christendom? Is not the incalculable wealth which they raked in through their false and fabricated purgatory sheer shameful robbery and thievery throughout the whole world? The incalculable wealth they have accumulated with their usurious masses and sacrificial masses, is it not sheer shameful robbery and thievery throughout the whole world? The incalculable wealth they procured through licenses to eat butter during Lent, through pilgrimages, the worship of the saints, and innumerable other deceptions, is it not sheer shameful robbery and thievery throughout the whole world? Where did the pope, cardinals, and bishops acquire kingdoms and principalities? How did they become the secular lords of all the world? Is it not entirely through their infinitely shameful robbery and thievery? What else are they than the greatest robbers and thieves on the face of the earth? And yet you find here no thought of repentance or restitution. Indeed, there is not enough good blood in their veins to enable them to administer their office a little, to give their possession of such property at least a slight semblance of honor. Instead, they condemn, revile, and persecute God's name, his word and work. And now they come and demand that you defend such thieves and robbers with your blood, so that they may not only go uncorrected but may also be encouraged to practice this kind of thing all the more. Consider what a great, mighty thief and rogue, robber and traitor you become and are if you assist and protect such robbers and thieves with your blood and life; for you will burden yourself with all of this and share in their guilt.

Then you must also burden yourself with all the blood the pope has shed, with all the murders and all the wars he has instigated, all the misery and grief he has caused throughout the world. Who can relate all the blood, murders, and wretchedness which the pope and his followers have occasioned? Some have computed that for the pope's sake alone eleven hundred thousand men have been slain since the papacy elevated itself above the empire. Some set the figure higher.

* * *

One might tolerate an evil life; but one can and must not tolerate, much less help to defend, a person who condemns doctrine and God's word and who elevates himself over God. They have disseminated so many doctrinal abominations within Christendom that these cannot be numbered. They repent of none of them, nor do they want to change them, but they openly defend them all and rigorously insist on being in the right. All of that would rest on your neck and conscience. You would make yourself a partner of all such abominations and you would be guilty if you helped to defend them. Let us mention just a few. How can your conscience bear the shameful, lying fraud of indulgences, with which they scandalously misled so many thousands of souls, yes, all of Christendom and all the world, deceiving them and defrauding them of their money and property? Yet they do not repent of this, nor do they intend to abrogate   this practice, although they are well aware of the great villainy they have committed thereby. They taught the people to place their trust in indulgences, and to die in that belief. This in itself is so atrocious and terrible that if they were otherwise as holy and pure as St. John the Baptist, they should properly be condemned to the depths of hell just for this; they should not be worthy that the earth bear them or the sun shine down on them, much less that we fight for them or defend them.

* * *

Furthermore, how will your conscience bear the blasphemous fraud of purgatory, with which they also treacherously duped and falsely frightened all the world and appropriated almost all its property and splendor by lying and thievery?   For with this they also completely extinguished that one and only comfort and trust in Christ and taught Christians to place their attention and expectation and reliance in the bequests which they trust will follow them.

* * *

Furthermore, you have to load yourself down with all the abominations and blasphemies they committed, and still daily commit, throughout the entire papacy with the dear mass, with buying and selling, and with innumerable other desecrations of the holy sacrament, in which they sacrifice God's Son to him continually as though they were better and holier than God's Son. They do not let the sacrament be a gift of God, to be received through faith, but convert it into a sacrifice and a work with which they atone for themselves and for other people and acquire all sorts of grace and aid.

* * *

Furthermore, how will you endure their terrible idolatries? It was not enough that they venerated the saints and praised God in them, but they actually made them into gods. They put that noble child, the mother Mary, right into the place of Christ. They fashioned Christ into a judge and thus devised a tyrant for anguished consciences, so that all comfort and confidence was transferred from Christ to Mary, and then everyone turned from Christ to his particular saint.

* * *

Again: How will your conscience endure the great evil, the torment, and the violence they have done to all the world by means of their agonizing confession? They have driven so many souls to despair with this and have deprived and robbed despondent consciences of all Christian comfort; for they concealed and hushed up the power of absolution and faith treacherously and maliciously and insisted solely on the intolerable torment and impossible toil of relating one's sins and of feeling contrition for them. They promised grace and salvation in return for such contrition and recounting of sin as our own work. Thus they pointed and directed us away from Christ to ourselves.

* * *

Furthermore, you must burden yourself with and aid the terrible, fraudulent, shameful tomfoolery of the devil which they have promoted with relics and pilgrimages, and which they by no means intend to discontinue. O God, how it has snowed and rained in this respect. What a sheer cloudburst of lies and fraud has broken upon us! How the devil extolled dead bones, garments, and utensils as the saints' limbs and utensils! How confidently people believed all the liars! How they flocked to join pilgrimages! All of this was approved by pope, bishops, priests, and monks; or at least, they said nothing and left the people in error and took their money and goods.

* * *

The third reason why you must refuse obedience to the emperor in such a call to arms is this: if you did otherwise you would not only burden yourself with all these abominations and help strengthen them, but you would also lend a hand in overthrowing and exterminating all the good which the dear gospel has again restored and established. For those villains are not satisfied with preserving such devilries and outrages; as the edict states, they will tolerate no changes but will eradicate and utterly destroy all that we have ever taught, lived for, and done, and still live for and do. This reason also encompasses a great deal; for our gospel has, thanks be to God, accomplished much good. Previously no one knew the real meaning of the gospel, Christ, baptism, confession, the sacrament [of the altar], faith, Spirit, flesh, good works, the Ten Commandments, the Our Father, prayer, suffering, comfort, temporal government, the state of matrimony, parents, children, masters, manservant, mistress, maidservant, devils, angels, world, life, death, sin, justice, forgiveness, God, bishop, pastor, church, a Christian, or the cross. In brief, we were totally ignorant about all that it is necessary for a Christian to know. All of this was obscured and suppressed by the popish asses. They are, as you know, just that— great, coarse, ignorant asses in Christian affairs. For I too was one, and I know that I am telling the truth on this matter. All devout hearts will bear witness to this; for they would gladly have been instructed about even one of these items, but they were held captive by the pope as I was and could gain neither the opportunity nor the permission to be instructed. We did not know otherwise than that priests and monks alone were everything, and that we relied on their works and not on Christ.

But now—praise be to God—it has come to pass that man and woman, young and old, know the catechism; they know how to believe, to live, to pray, to suffer, and to die. Consciences are well instructed about how to be Christians and how to recognize Christ. We preach the truth about faith and good works. In brief, the aforementioned items have again come to light, and pulpit, altar, and baptismal font have been restored to their proper place, so that—thank God—the form of a Christian church can again be recognized. But you will have to assist in the extermination and destruction of all of this if you fight for the papists. For they will not tolerate that any of these doctrines should be taught and established by us, but, as they say, they want to restore the *status quo ante*, the old state of things, and not permit a single change. You will have to help burn all the German books, New Testaments, psalters, prayer books, hymnals, and all the good things we wrote, and which they themselves admit to be good. You will have to help keep everyone ignorant about the Ten Commandments, the Lord's Prayer, and the Creed; for this is the way it used to be. You will have to help keep everyone from learning anything about baptism, the sacrament, faith, government, matrimony, or the gospel. You will have to help keep everyone from knowing Christian liberty. You will have to help keep people from placing their trust in Christ and deriving their comfort from him. For all of that was non-existent before; all of it is something new.

Furthermore, you will have to help to condemn and disgrace the children of our pastors and preachers, poor forsaken orphans, as the children of whores. You will have to help people to rely again on the works of monks and priests instead of on Christ, and on buying their merits and their cowls for the hour of death. You will have to help them fill Christendom again with whoring, adultery, and other unnatural, shameful vices, instead of getting married. You will have to help restore the atrocious carnival of the sacrificial mass. You will have to help in the defense of all their avarice, robbery, and thievery, by means of which they acquire their riches. But why should I enlarge on this? You will have to help in the destruction of Christ's word and his whole kingdom and in the rebuilding of the kingdom of the devil. For that is the aim of the scoundrels who are bent on restoring the *status quo ante,* the old state of things. They are of the Antichrist, or Counter-Christ; therefore they can only do what is against Christ, especially in the cardinal doctrine according to which our heart is to look to Christ alone for consolation and assurance and not to look to our own works; that is, we are to be delivered from sin and to be justified by faith alone, as is written in Romans 10 [:10], "For man believes with his heart and so is justified."

This doctrine, I say, they will not tolerate under any circumstances. We are able to forego it just as little; for if this doctrine vanishes, the church vanishes.

* * *

These things I wanted to say to my dear Germans by way of warning. And as I did above, I testify here again that I do not wish to incite or spur anyone to war or rebellion or even self-defense, but solely to peace. But if the papists—our devil—refuse to keep the peace and, impenitently raging against the Holy Spirit with their persistent abominations, insist on war, and thereby get their heads bloodied or even perish, I want to witness publicly here that this was not my doing, nor did I give any cause for it. It is

NOTES

NOTES

35 "Colleges": The word "college" here denotes a corporation of clergy supported by a foundation and performing certain religious services.

38 "Pretense at reformation": Three "reform councils" had been convened during the fifteenth century. The Council of Pisa (1409) was convened by cardinals to resolve the schism caused by two rival popes. The result was the election of a third pontiff. The Council of Constance (1414-1418) successfully deposed the three rival popes and elected Martin V. It was at this council that John Huss was condemned and burned at the stake. The Council of Basel (1431-1439) was characterized by hostility between the council and Pope Eugene IV, who excommunicated its members and convened a countercouncil, attended by the emperor, at Ferrara (1438). The council which remained at Basel deposed Eugene and elected Felix V. Unable to find political support and recognition, Felix resigned within ten months of his election.

38 "A young . . . head of state": Charles V, who had been elected emperor in 1519 when only twenty years of age, and whom Luther appeared before at the Diet of Worms in 1521.

38 "Julius II": Pope Julius II (1503-1513) was notorious for his unscrupulous use of political power. Continually involved in war, he led his armies in person and was "the scourge of Italy."

41 *"Characteres indelebiles"*: The *character indelebiles*, or "indelible mark," was given authoritative formulation in the bull *Exultate Deo* (1439). Eugene IV, summing up the decrees of the Council of Florence, wrote: "Among these sacraments there are three—baptism, confirmation, and orders—which indelibly impress upon the soul a character, i.e., a certain spiritual mark which distinguishes them from the rest" (Carl Mirbt, *Quellen zur Geschichte des Papstums* [2nd ed.], No. 150).

43 "Under interdict": The interdict prohibits the administration of the sacraments and the other rites of the church within a given territory. Its use was not uncommon in the Middle Ages, and at the height of papal power it proved an effective means of bringing rulers to terms.

Page

47 *"Conciliabulum"*: A mere gathering of people as opposed to a *concilium*, i.e., a valid council.

55 "Postils": The Postils were a collection of sermons expounding the Epistles and Gospels for the Sundays and festivals of the church year.

63 "Frogs must have their storks": The proverb means in effect: "like people, like prince" according to Karl F. Wander (ed.), *Deutsches Sprichwörter-Lexikon* (5 vols.; Leipzig: Brockhaus, 1867-1880), I, 1230, *"Frosch,"* No. 34. It derives from the Aesop fable about the frogs who insisted on having a king, and were finally granted a stork who devoured them all.

72 "False teachers and prophets": Luther has several in mind. Thomas Münzer (ca. 1490-1525) was a native of Stolberg in the Harz Mountains. After a rather unsettled career including duty as confessor in a convent, he became a preacher of radical religious and social reform. His incitement of the peasants and workers of Mühlhausen (Thuringia) led to their severe defeat in the battle of Frankenhausen. Nicholas Storch was leader of the Zwickau prophets, who were responsible for fomenting the Wittenberg riots of 1522 when Luther was in exile at the Wartburg. Andrew Bodenstein Karlstadt had been Luther's colleague at the University of Wittenberg, but like Münzer represented a completely independent direction of thought. He supported the Wittenberg riots and was banished by Luther after the disturbances had been quieted. Karlstadt generally was held responsible for the unrest among the Franconian peasants.

87 "Submit the case to judgment": In other words, a ruler need not wait for a judicial verdict against the peasants.

112 "Devil! . . . St. Quirinus!": These expletive invocations of the saints call upon them to afflict with the malady whose cure popular piety attributed to them: St. Vitus, epilepsy; St. Anthony, an inflamed condition of the skin; and St. Quirinus, the plague. Cf. Helen Roeder, *Saints and Their Attributes* (London, New York, Toronto, 1955), pp. 32, 62, 102, 115, 221.

122 "Endowing masses": Endowed masses were generally said for the benefit of deceased persons who had made testamentary provision for them.

123 "Pallia, annates": The pallium, or woolen shoulder cape, is the emblem of the archepiscopal office. It had to be secured from Rome. Luther charged that the pallium (and the office it signified)

was for sale at exorbitant prices. Originally the annates were the income received by a bishop from vacant benefices in his diocese. The right to this income was subsequently claimed by the papacy.

128 "Confess and teach his gospel": Matt. 10:32. Christians under Turkish rule were not permitted to organize congregations. The use of bells was prohibited and conversion to Christianity was punishable by death.

129 "I cannot expect any miracle": Luther regarded the lifting of the siege of Vienna in October, 1529, as a miracle.

130 *"Cruciata"*: The Crusades.

136 *"Aliud est invasor, aliud transgressor"*: "An invader is one thing, a transgressor is another."

137 "Little kitten . . . company": When a cat washed itself it was supposed to mean that guests were coming. Luther uses this proverb in the sense of putting on a false front.